What you think is weird
is weirder than you think.
                              -Tenney

VOLUME ONE • 2010 - 2019

THEORETICAL
WEIRDO

A MISH MASH OF RAMBLINGS ABOUT WEIRDNESS

JOHN E.L. TENNEY

A MISH MASH OF RAMBLINGS ABOUT WEIRDNESS

THEORETICAL
WEIRDO

JOHN E.L. TENNEY

ISBN: 9798637935222

TABLE OF CONTENTS

OPENING RAMBLE

This book begins with an apology.

"I'm sorry."

My mind is a disorganized file cabinet of information, thoughts, and ever-changing ideas. If you have ever had the opportunity to see one of my "lectures" you'll quickly recognize my meandering and hyperventilating changes in narrative and context. There is too much information in my head and it comes out in ways which I cannot control. That being said, have fun with this nonsense.

The biggest problem with writing a book is writing it. You never know if a story, or idea, which is told over coffee, is going to be as enthralling or exciting after it's been locked down forever onto the printed page. For me this is an enormous challenge. I love talking to people, exchanging stories, constructing ideas with others, and I can't help but worry that once these pages have shipped to the printer I will remember some crucial element that would have made all the difference in how a story will be understood by the reader.

As bookstore shelves overflow with titles dealing with ghosts, hauntings, ghost-hunting and associated "paranormal" phenomena I can relax in the hopes that if this book is terrible it will be lost in the "speculation" section drown in a the sea of titles that I believe to be boorish, poorly researched and almost always nightmarishly designed.

Yeah, I said it. Most of those books are awful …really, they're awful.

I feel the need to more clearly explain why I take such a hard stance against a community to which I am mostly ashamed to belong to so I shall.

I have always been a passionate individual. I stand up for my ideas, will fight for a cause and will challenge those who wish to be challenged. My upbringing made me this way. I'm stubborn, critical and sometimes to a fault, honest. I brought all of these character flaws and strengths with me when I made the choice to investigate ideas and concepts that challenge our everyday world.

The researchers, educators, and investigators that helped me to become an answer-seeker taught me that no matter how hard you work you can always do better. So when I am confronted with "paranormal-researchers" who proclaim that they are awakening society to the existence of a new understand of who we are, how the universe works, and the role human-beings play in that universe, I can only wonder if they will be taken seriously – especially if they are wearing a Ghost Busters T-shirt. Can they truly believe that the answers to the mysteries of life and death are made more palatable by using "bloody" fonts on their books, banners, and websites? How can a group that is seriously investigating, what is generally referred to as, paranormal phenomena use paranormal phenomena (psychics, remote viewing) to prove itself? If I am lost in the forest I cannot ask myself for directions out of it.

Today's researchers of supernatural phenomena must never forget the diligence of the investigators who have come before them. Too many times, information – which may hold a breakthrough in the serious search for answers in a field that is most often not taken seriously – can fall to the wayside forever. The pioneers of psychical research may be forgotten by people who have only a mild curiosity in heterotical studies, but learned women and men of the past should never be struck from the thoughts of those, in our shared field, who would now call themselves "professionals." Hundreds of thousands of pages have been written, tens of thousands of case studies have been made, and the ramifications of that hard work should be recognized as the important legacy we as researchers have been left to uphold. The manner in which we choose to treat the work of those who came before us will determine how we will be viewed in the future. This is not a psychic prediction; it is a fact.

In this book you find a brief sampling of my stories, ideas, ramblings and thoughts. These small glimpses into the mess of my mind should in many cases seem benign or trite. I do not consider myself one of the world's leading thinkers. I am simply a person who for whatever reason has dedicated my life to thought-exploring the nature of reality. From paranormal investigation techniques to demons, from Bigfoot to our spaceship Moon I have tried to compile a seemingly untraceable, mishmash of blips on my intellectual radar. Hopefully you will find something of value or a least a cinder which sets aflame a better idea.

Over the decades I have had the pleasure, and sometimes the misfortune, to interview and befriend a large variety of people who believe they have been in contact with beings from beyond our world. The majority of these people are kind, thoughtful, intelligent persons who are having some type of experience that they cannot fully explain or prove. Of course there are certain individuals who many would consider "crazy," or at the very least, simply attention seekers. No matter how weird their stories may be I cannot help but be fascinated by them. Sometimes the "facts" included in the story, by the experiencer, are far-fetched, ill-formed and, to our current understanding, scientifically impossible. Other stories are benign, not so exciting and seem somewhat plausible though startling in their implications.

If the tales told by most individuals are total fabrications, as long as no one was hurt or bilked out of their lunch money, I am fine with these stories. If nothing happened to these persons, except the creation of a simple plan to trick people into talking to them, I am also fine with that.

Nothing in many of these experiences seems meant to hurt. In fact, many of the tales I've been told speak of beautifully peaceful worlds whose citizens love and adore nature, and each other. Planets populated by people much like us– but kinder, more compassionate, and willing to help those who cannot help themselves. The people in these stories are much like us, but also very different. They are far more caring. I am also fine with stories, whether true or not, about people like that.

This book is a collection of thoughts. Some of these thoughts have appeared on my website, some have been spoken at lectures, many have been whispered in private but all of them have spent time rattling around my head fueled by caffeine and my unending marvel of the universe. These thoughts are meant to be seeds. My goal has always been to construct larger ideas with those around me; ideas that I alone could not create. There is a hint of altruism in my thoughts but, in most cases, I am hoping to seed ideas in various minds so that at a later date, after they have grown, they can be fed back to me.

Everything you will read in the follow pages were culled for lecture notes, blog posts, tweets and thoughts from the year 2010 through 2019. I have not altered them in anyway in order to update them. I have left them as they were originally written as a testament to how I then thought. I've also made the choice to only correct spelling errors if I felt they interfered with factual information such as names and places. I think it's important every now and again to see the failings of humans including spelling errors.

We take for granted just how precious our lives are. The day-to-day grind of paying bills, making ends meet, non-stop rushing to-and-fro filling our moments with the endless minutia of "normalcy" drowns our days until we suddenly realize it's time to go. So when another of my human family tells me a short, wonderful story of weirdness, when they ruminate on marvelous mysteries, I'll take some time to listen.

There is enough death and destruction, hatred and anger, in this life for everyone. Sometimes we just need to sit back, relax and let all of the creativity and high-strangeness of the universe unwind in front of us, because you never really know ...and it just might all be true.

John E.L. Tenney

GONE TODAY HEAR TOMORROW

Over the passed decades spent researching anomalistic phenomena one thing has become certain, there is not a lot of certainty. The inherent problems with researching that which is considered by most to be "unknown" is very much limited by what we think we "know" and how directly related what is known to the unknown we research. Whew.

Do digital cameras have a better chance at revealing "ghostly" manifestations or are film cameras the better option? Does analog audio tape more adequately reproduce the voices of the unseen world due to its influenceability by electromagnetic fields or are the chip-sets in digital recorders more sensitive to the "spirit" world? Questions like these, and others like them, have been bandied about for decades and although more "scientific" research may show one form of investigation producing better "results" than another one we should always be prepared to either reclassify collected data if not relegating it to the file cabinet in the basement or, if need be, the trash can.

When we speak about, or construct ideas dealing with, what is commonly called, Electronic Voice Phenomena we quickly become aware of the multitude of camps that people belong to. Some people believe that any type of recording device will disclose words from the after-world while others are staunchly convinced that only the right type of devices will reveal our mysterious speakers. Of course these voices which many believe to be paranormal very often play their part by refusing to conform to any specific testing.

When I say this I know it will draw controversy from the groups that have "figured out" how these voices can manifest yet I say it because we bear witness to it happening. Saying paranormal phenomena like EVP conforms to certain rules and only will only work in a certain manner, at this point, leads to a slippery slope. The Earth may have been believed flat for centuries but it never really was and those who challenged the idea were scorn and ridiculed for thinking to the contrary.

We see a great example of science accepting various ideas in one form with the concept of wave-particle duality. The principle of complementarity, (that some articles may have various properties which appear to be contradictory) in physics is one that all researchers, paranormal researchers included, should find fascinating as it begins to allow a more fluid structure to the ideas we try and discuss. The assumption that because some of our scientific ideas work for us right now, so they must apply forever to everything for all times, is heavy-handed at best and bigoted at worst. Science is a method of inquiry not a dogmatic belief structure.

To "do science" is to experiment, test, falsify, challenge, reproduce and is often times tedious and, for most non-scientists, boring. People who say they are involved in researching supernatural phenomena in a "scientific manner" are usually not doing so; but they say it because it sounds cool to other researchers. To say that anomalous voices are only one thing, (only and always a wave never a particle), can not only discourage research in new directions but on a more personal note can create animosity between researchers who are all trying with the resources available to explain this mystifying universe in which we live.

If need be, new, linguistic terms should be created for the various structures of paranormal research. Words are immmmportant to the exchange and construction of ideas and the paranormal field is limited in its vocabulary for describing the experiences had by those involved.

When we hear or say the word "ghost" what do we mean? Not all ghostly manifestations portray themselves in the same manner; is a poltergeist different from a transmissive visitant? What do we even mean by transmissive visitant?* It does seem that there are various types of EVP – some that are created through the movement and change of air pressure resulting in an audible voice while another is generated solely by the fluctuations in electromagnetic fields, still others seem to be only generated with the assistance of a carrier wave or background noise. And, while all of these may be considered by one person or another as auditory apophenia they still should each be given a distinct term by which they can be referenced. As an example:

EVP: Electronic Voice Phenomena – The broad umbrella term for the research and investigation of anomalous sounds and voices caught through the usage of electronic technology. The term remains in use due to its widespread and long-term usage. It lacks specificity and therefore can be used in a general manner.

BVP: Bearing Voice Phenomena – This term makes specific that the sounds were recorded by way of a carrier wave, noise generator, white/pink noise or other physical audio medium.

DVP: Discernible Voice Phenomena – This is a voice or sound which is actually heard by the human ear and can as any audible sound be recorded.

AVP: Alternated Voice Phenomena - This applies to a seemingly intelligent and responsive voice captured using machines and equipment which reappropriate already known sounds such as radios and televisions. This term is used also when performing sessions with equipment which have embedded within them internal word dictionaries.

EMVP: Electromagnetic Voice Phenomena – This term applies to any sound which is not registered by the human hear but is recorded via the transmission of electromagnetism.

I by no means think that these terms should be used but the community of researchers who are currently engaged in the research of anomalistic phenomena should at some point begin to classify with a more specific language of what they are doing.

Hopefully by creating a useful and more intense lexicon we will cut down on confusion and quell in-fighting. It will also assist the field down its path to being recognized as a more serious. I know many people scoff that words are as influence-able as I make them out to be but just think of the damage done, to our shared field of interest, by the word "Ghostbuster" and you'll see just how much words make a difference... after all, isn't a large part of EVP itself really just trying to make sense of words?

By the way, earlier in this writing I spelled "important" incorrectly on purpose.

*Transmissive Visitant: An alleged visitor from the non-corporeal world that can allow the transmission of energy, in any of its forms, into the realm of human experiences.

WHAT'S IN A NAME? A QUICK THOUGHT ON DEMONOLOGY AND DEMONOLOGISTS

As the paranormal community becomes larger, and seemingly more outrageous, there have been quite a number of people who have recently started to refer to themselves as "Demonologists". Now, I understand they believe that since they study "demonology," the title fits. But we should remember that historically "demonology" and "demonologists" have little to do with each other.

Demonology is exactly what it sounds like, the study of demons or the beliefs about them. This study is first and foremost to include any and all alleged demons regardless of the theological system that they belong to. Not only does "Demonology" study "demons," but it studies demonic forces in all of their supposed manifestations including familiars, egregores, ancestor worship, fallen angels and animal spirits to name a few. Most so-called "Demonologists" are focused on traditional Judeo-Christian demons & devils while forgetting that there are recognized demons throughout history that many believe to have been in existence long before the rise of Christianity.

The largest and most disturbing point, to me, is that the term "Demonologist" now refers to those who study demons. The usage of the word in this form is relatively modern.

Historically, a Demonologist was a "witch-hunter" or someone who exposed persons who were believed to be in league with demonic forces. Traditional Demonologists such as Remy, Sinistrari, Bodin and Valderama, to name a few, were more than incidentally responsible for causing such a panic about witchcraft that hundreds, perhaps thousands of innocent people were put to death. I point this out because it, to me, shows a total disregard for the past. People heard the word "Demonology" and started calling themselves "Demonologists" without any care or concern that they had just associated themselves with some of the most closed-minded and vindictive people in our history.

There have been people who, back in the 1970's, tried to reclaim the title of "Demonologist" as something which meant "a fighter of the demonic" but the word was, I assume, mostly used because it was looked good on a book cover. We must keep in mind the idea of devils and demons was reintroduced to the general public by way of the movies The Exorcist and The Amityville Horror. A very easy way to sell books and make a name for yourself was, at the time, to associate yourself with those very popular films. The word "Demon" evokes the nerve-centers at the heart of the belief systems of millions so why not name yourself as fighter of demons? Why not? Because the word is wrong.

I know that the word "Demonologist" makes etymological sense but we must remember that the word existed before our modern day usage and it had a meaning, and that history makes a difference. If you believed in national social programs such as public schools, post offices, the highway system, etc. You would never say you agreed with Nazi philosophy. The word Nazi means National Socialism, but the historical context of the word keeps you from calling yourself a Nazi. History matters.

The historically recognized Demonologists of the 1600's and 1700's repeated anecdotal stories and rumors without basing any of their charges on facts. They were truly the demonic evil that they themselves believed they were unmasking.

"But, it's only a word."
Well, I say words matter. History matters.

The fact is this, Demonologists were simple-minded, frightened people who helped to murder innocent people. Even if you believe you are a "Demonologist," I will not call you one; I wouldn't hang that title on my worst enemy.

ATTACKED! THE DEMON OF JUDGEMENT!

Many years ago, upon my first visit to a client's home and within moments of entering, I felt a strange, even disturbing presence. There was a screaming that can only be described as horrific. Everyone heard the sound. Try as we might, we could not stop the almost inhuman wailing. It continued throughout the course of my interview with the clients and at many times interrupted our conversation due to an increase in volume and intensity.

At one point I was scratched across my arm to the point of needing antiseptic and bandages immediately. While I was in the bathroom cleaning the newly received wound, one of the clients was violently kicked while the other had to dodge a small vase of flowers that was thrown from across the kitchen and into the living room.

Still the interview continued.

The table at which we were sitting began to shake until all of our cups of coffee were spilled. One of the saucers shattered when it fell from the table and onto the floor.

The interview continued.

The screaming began again, at which time blankets and pillows that had been lying on the couch were tossed from one side of the room to the other. In the kitchen, the cupboards were opened and slammed shut. Pots and pans flew from the kitchen down the hallway until one particularly large pan smashed through the glass window of the back screen door.

It was at this point, seeing the exasperation of the clients, that I excused myself for the night and made my way home.

Throughout the entire drive home I couldn't help but wonder how I would deal with the situation had that home been mine, and how I would act if I had children with such "bratty" dispositions.

Did I mention that it was their children who were causing all of the disruptions?

Over the years I have been kicked, punched, bitten, had objects thrown at me. I've been told to "go die" and "I hate you" by children; most people have. None of those children were evil. None of those children were "demons". Most of the time those children, for whatever reason, were scared, frustrated, confused, lonely, desperate for attention or just badly behaved. Sometimes they were just being kids.

How do you know a "ghost" is evil? Or that something is "demonic"? Is it because of what is happening, or is it because of what you think is happening?

In our daily interactions with other human beings we can easily mistake frustration with anger or sadness with hate, and that happens with people with whom we can easily communicate, people we can see, people who can tell us what is really going on in their lives.

As of right now, we do not have that ability with those who have "passed on."

So before we jump onto the bandwagon of fear and join in the circus of the demonic, we should take the time to realize we really don't know what is happening and we shouldn't be so quick to judge others, even if they are unseen.

DEMONS FOR BELIEVERS

This article is for everyone but written specifically to be read by those who, mostly because of popular media, now believe in demons.

Many years ago I had the pleasure of chatting with theologian and former Jesuit Fr. Malachi Martin. We discussed his history working with the Vatican's Biblical Institute, conspiracy theories surrounding the Vatican and of course exorcisms. A warm and open conversation was had about topics that at the time, and probably to some today, the general public would, I believe, have found unbelievable.

Now, due to the influence of reality TV and the extreme overexposure of so-called demonic forces by popular films and books the concepts of a "demonic reality" are thought about by many and believed by many more. I remember discussing the various types of "demonic" attacks that Fr. Martin explained as possible; from general psychological harassment, alcohol/substance abuse to actual possession of the human body by a non-human force. We disagreed and agreed with each other on many points during the conversation but ultimately left each other smiling.

Fr. Martin has now passed away and I am left with only the memories of our conversations and ideas which have over the years matured and expanded. For that I am forever grateful. Yet, over those years the ideas and conversations have allowed me a unique opportunity to watch the general public's discourse regarding demonic influences on our world evolve and unfortunately in most cases degenerate.

Frustratingly it becomes more and more difficult to explain and discuss the issue of demonic possession in a serious, philosophical, academic and non-hyperbolic way when in truth the squeakiest wheel does actually gets the grease. Reality television is not the home of the intelligent and insightful exchanging of information that we need. There are people now in the public eye who without any, or very little, care or concern for how they portray themselves or certain situations continue to promote wild-eyed tales of fancy for the sole purpose of gaining larger viewership or selling more merchandise. These people seem to have no regard for how the general viewing audiences may internalize what is being shown and how influential psychologically these "true" events can be not only to the young but also to the "true believers." To say it is a disservice is nothing more than apathy.

It is nonsense and insulting.

Demons, demonic influences and possessions can be discussed in a serious manner and lead to larger philosophical questions about the natural world around us and an alleged all-permeating supernatural reality. The topic of demonic influences help to make shocking films and startling TV but, (this is stressed for the true believer of things paranatural), think about who and how the conversation is influenced.

How did the topic become so popular?
Why are there now far more reported cases?
Who are the famous, wealthy, successful people who promote the outrageous?
Who holds sway over the masses with a blend of shock and fear?

And while you are considering questions like the ones above please keep in mind how alleged demonic influences supposedly work.

Not all who are "possessed" are drooling, screaming tortured souls. Indeed religious officials charged with performing exorcisms will tell you that the reason there is such a reaction is that the person who is allegedly possessed is intensely fighting against the possession. But what about those who do not feel the need to fight? What about those who want to be possessed?

One of the topics Fr. Martin and I discussed all those many years ago were the examples of "perfect possession." This is a topic, like many others, which has been left behind in our 24-hour-basic cable FacebookTwitterInstagramGoogle Universe.

The discussion of the people who want to be possessed. The people who for whatever reason whether it be the gain of fame or money allow themselves to be a conduit for purposeful misinformation and hysterical confusion of the masses. In Fr. Martin's mind the most diabolically possessed person is the person who has made an "agreement" with the "thing" which possesses him or her. These people seem absolutely normal and yet they are not. Again, Fr. Martin believed that these were the most frightening of cases the most horrific these were people who have "sold their souls".

Now I ask you, the believers, these questions in seriousness.

Who is benefiting from your hysteria?
Who is using fear to gain your confidence?
Who takes the darkest most repellent aspects of religious ideas and uses it for self-promotion?
Do you believe in those people?
Do you support those people?

Because truthfully, anyone who tries to influence your life through the promotion of fear and darkness... is a demon.

THE WORLD'S MOST HAUNTED LOCATION

I am very frequently asked by people, "Where is the most haunted place in the world?" My answer is always the same, "If any place is haunted, it's the Earth."

Now, although many people think that I am trying to be funny, which I am, I am also being serious. So, let's try a little thought experiment.

If ghosts are what people generally believe them to be, the remaining energy/consciousness of a human being who has died, then each person could potentially become a ghost when they pass out of this realm.

I'm bad with math but I can make this easy on myself and you…so hold on.

Since human beings have been "human beings", (we'll just go with the genus Homo which will put us around two million years ago), estimates of population would show that approximately 75 to 105 billion humans have been born and died on planet Earth. Now, let's say that some "ghosts" have passed on and or perhaps never became ghosts; I'll be generous here and say that out of the 100 billion deaths 85% either never became ghosts or are ghosts that have moved into a different sphere of existence which doesn't interact with us on Earth. That leaves us with approximately 15 billion ghosts still residing with us on this planet.

Now that we know we might have as many as 15 billion "ghostly" friends wandering around we need to look at where they could be. The total land surface area of Earth is about 57 million square miles, of which about 57% is uninhabitable leaving us with about 15 billion acres of land where people have lived and died and therefore would be places consider to be "hauntable".

See why I was so generous by saying 85% of the ghosts are "gone"? It makes it easy for me to do the math.

So, 15 billion ghosts divided by 15 billion acres of land equals one ghost per acre… at least.

The possibility, if ghosts are even real, is that my numbers are wildly off in either direction. If there are 30 billion ghosts then you have two spectral friends in every acre or perhaps you have hundreds or thousands jammed up in one acre but zero in the acre next door. Perhaps there are only a billion ghosts so you'd only have one ghost every quarter of a mile. Either way if ghosts are real and hanging around they are everywhere. Earth really is the most haunted place on Earth.

This idea of billions of potential ghosts doesn't even include if animals have ghosts. If animals and insects can become ghosts then we are surrounded on all sides.

So why are people traveling all over the world to investigate ghosts?

Isn't there at least one right next to you?

Also, if you ever feel a weird itch... spider ghosts.
Billions of spider ghosts.

COME AT ME GHOST!
THREE REASONS "PROVOKING" MIGHT NOT BE SO GREAT

Over the years the big fad in ghost hunting, not research, is the process commonly being called "provocation." Hundreds of ghost hunters and dozens of groups proclaim "provoking" as one of the best ways to get some kind of response from residents of the after-realm. Since our shared field of interest is speculative in nature, I shall speculate on three ways that "provoking" might NOT be the best way to "hunt" ghosts.

3. No ears.

If you believe in ghosts you probably believe that they do not have a physical body such as our own. If that is true and ghosts (entities, spirits, etc.) are not corporeal, then they do not have ears as we do. Without ears, the process that makes living people hear sound as uttered by lips while air is pushed out of lungs and through the throat creating vibrations which are received by the ear translated into sound and then deciphered by the brain as words is not the process by which a ghost would hear us. No ears, no sound. But they seem to be "hearing," so there may be some other process taking place. If they are not hearing our words, perhaps they are only receiving the impression of our words as we speak them through some sort of psychical means that we are currently unaware of. In the case of "ghosts" picking up our thoughts, not our actual words, then why would it matter if we were screaming them or whispering them? On many occasions over the last 20+ years I have conducted ITC experiments where I simply thought my questions without any verbalization at all, yet I have still received replies. I'll dive into this concept in a later chapter.

2. Provoking is rude.

That's right, rude. Although "ghost hunters" like to think that they know who or what spirits they are trying to communicate with, we have no proof as to who or what the spirits really are. So standing in a room shouting and being mean to someone you don't even know is simply rude. Grow up and stop bullying, we're trying to do research here.

1. Leftovers.

Another theory of "ghost hunters" is that some sort of energy generated by strong personalities or traumatic events can be leftover after a person dies. Well, following that train of "logic" we would assume that the energy could be leftover by anyone in a strong emotional state – even "ghost hunters." What if a group of people goes to an allegedly haunted location and two or three of them get themselves worked up and start "provoking"? Can we be sure that after those "ghost hunters" leave, they haven't left some of that energy behind? So the next weekend when someone goes to that same location and they start to "feel" a presence, it could possibly be the energy leftover from the people that were there last week. Imagine a place like Waverly Hills that has been filled with people screaming, running, yelling, laughing all the time. Do you think none of that energy has been left behind?

I've tried "provoking" myself and have been unimpressed with the results. The only thing I've ever seen "provoking" actually do is increase a television show's ratings… and raise my blood pressure.

SOME THOUGHTS AND A CHALLENGE

Being a person who investigates phenomena — which is commonly referred to as "paranormal" — is not as easy as some people would have you think. To begin with, many people think you are insane, simple-minded, easily fooled, mentally unhinged and/or just plain dumb. Once you get past the personal attacks you may, frustratingly, find that you have just dedicated a large amount of your very limited life to researching a subject whose focus may never be able to be concretely proven to be true. None the less, you continue with your work knowing that the time and energy you've expended has, hopefully, gone to further the knowledge of the entire human race on what is unquestionably the largest question known to any person throughout all of history.

Many individuals who delve into the world of psychical, paranormal, supernatural phenomena become caught up with the technology. They spend countless hours listening to audio recordings, studying video footage and checking electromagnetic fields. Of course these aspects of investigation are important in and of the fact that they can become part of a larger data set which may someday be collected and catalogued along with information gathered by other researchers which could eventually answer some of the questions surrounding the associated phenomena.

In recent decades, due in part to the advancement of technology, paranormal research has lost one of the most important aspects of itself, the underlying philosophical discussions.

The first "haunted" house I ever personally encountered was in 1986 in my hometown of Royal Oak, Michigan. I was told that strange, unexplainable happenings were occurring in the house and I was asked to investigate. But, why me? It wasn't a question I asked because I was afraid; it was a question I asked because I couldn't understand why I was qualified to investigate a "haunted" house. I had never "ghost hunted," or the more popularly coined term of the time, "busted" a ghost. I was only 15 years old and all I had ever done was read and thought about paranormal phenomena.

Those were the reasons I was asked to do the investigation. I had spent years actually thinking about the how, what and whys of our weird world. Needless to say, that juvenile, terribly executed investigation led to a larger and more involved fascination that continues up to this very writing.

I have never been a very physically active person, in that, I never played sports and I don't run marathons. I have always been "bookish". I love reading. Maybe it was Michigan's winters that created a climate of introversion in me that eventually developed into introspection. Reading exercised my imagination and intellect. As those dual aspects of my personality developed I learned that deep reflection of known concepts could lead to a deeper understanding of the unknown. This philosophical approach to paranormal research is where I consider most of the work that needs to be done by researchers to be. Yet as movies, television and the internet grow in their proliferation, as sources of information become vast and easily accessible it seems as though the introspective concept of research has vanished.

People now just ask questions and wait for someone else to answer through a forum, text message or basic cable documentary. No one is even trying to think of new answers to these old questions. There's no time to think, there are too many "haunted" houses to investigate. And since there are now hundreds of thousands of researchers, one of them "must know" the answer.

I know that there will be some people who say that the above portrayal of researchers is thoughtless and saying that philosophical discussions have "vanished" is either sour grapes on my part or driven by my own ego. To those people I offer a challenge. It is the same challenge to which I have devoted my life and work.

Think more deeply and more creatively. Discuss new ideas, construct concepts within your own mind and test those ideas against the fire of others who are thinking as deeply and honestly as you are.

I declare that what the field of paranormal research needs is a philosophical side, or phanosophical, if there must be a specific term.

We must realize that although we sometimes are trying to figure out what a wispy cloud in a photograph is, or what an ill-defined voice on a recording is saying, what we are ultimately trying to do is answer the most intense and world-changing question our humankind has ever or will ever know, the question of what happens when we die?

ABOUT THE LEGENDS OF THE ORIGINAL INHABITANTS OF AMERICA

Just as the basis of every other culture's legends and myths have been lost to antiquity, so have the tales of the original inhabitants of North America. Who are we to say what is real and what is not?

As our knowledge of the universe increases with each scientific development and breakthrough, we have begun the process of quickly disregarding the stories of those who have come before us. We have never seen a man transform into a wolf, and indeed, science tells us it is an impossibility. Yet the underlying concept of "wild people," or humans that act in an animalistic manner, has simply been re categorized under the heading of "mental illness."

The tales told by the original North Americans are some of the most colorful and curious you may stumble upon. With deep reflection, they allow the modern reader to speculate about the actual events which may have created the legends in the first place. Our society is rife with re-imaginings of ancient tales told by similar cultures. Many people believe that the ancient Egyptians were in contact with beings from outer space and that the South American Maya received their mathematics and astronomy from our space brethren. One thing is certain in the legends recounted to us; the original inhabitants of North America had no issue educating their communities with the knowledge that "Sky People" did exist and very often interacted with the Earth's people.

When a person in our society weaves a fantastic tale of alien abduction or claims to have seen a flying object from another world, many may balk at the claims. But there are also those who wonder if there may be a scientific basis for the experience. I invite you to wonder, in the same manner, about the stories told by the former inhabitants of this land.

Their stories of spirits and unknown creatures, reveal that some beliefs of people hundreds of years ago are not so different than those held by many today. As a specific example, in the community of modern people intrigued by paranormal phenomena, the concept of "Shadow Persons" is one that creates heated debates between its adherents. Yet "shadow people" were discussed and known to the Blackfeet centuries ago. They believed that a person's shadow was his or her soul and that if a person led a wicked life they were not allowed to move into the after-world and were confined to this world as wanderers envying the living and seeking to do harm. This is what many "paranormal researchers" still believe to this day. The more things change...

Sure, the ideas presented in these stories may be, and probably are, just the fanciful imaginative explanations of natural processes by people who did not have access to the scientific advancements we current have. At the same time, they are stories created by people who were more emotionally and psychologically in touch with their surrounding world. Our modern world is more technologically advanced - this is not doubted - but it is also filled with the endless errand running, bill paying and information overload that has separated us from the wondrous natural experiences of the planet that is our shared home. It was not a simpler time - your chances of being eaten by a bear have significantly decreased - but it was a time that allowed deeper introspective reflection.

No one can say for sure that the Thunder men of the Passamaquoddy were or were not extraterrestrial visitors. When a star or cloud containing people lowers itself from the sky, we can only wonder if the foundation of the story actually contained an unknown flying vehicle. If a great horned serpent appeared on the shore of California tomorrow it might be shocking, but we would classify, categorize, add it to our current knowledge base and move on to the next great discovery... unless the creature also spoke - that might shock and startle a few scientists.

There are endless documentaries and books about ancient extraterrestrials and their influence on humankind. The tales and legends of the original North Americans seem to have been pushed to the back of the crowd. Perhaps it is because they did not leave behind massive stone structures or pictograms that can only be seen from outer space, or maybe there is a more serious and embarrassing reason.

The continent of North America was once populated by creative, beautiful people who saw themselves as children of the world, and they were systematically destroyed in a variety of ways. As European and Latin cultures "discovered" a new world, they made sure that not only did the stories, cultures and gods of the original inhabitants vanish, but also the people themselves. This destruction of cultures, of course, did not happen 4,000 or 5,000 years ago, and the conquering people are not some long ago civilization that has also, since that time, vanished. It's easy to speculate on the legends and stories of the Sumerians; due to the antiquity of their culture, we have no real point of reference. But there can be many uncomfortable emotions when discussing the beliefs of a people that still exists, through their own tenacity and fortitude, after a recent attempt in some cases to purposefully vanish them from the face of the Earth.

As modern Americans, many of us spend vacations and weekends visiting buildings that are 100 or 200 years old. We desire a connection to an ancient history in such a degree that any object over a century in age tends to be kept behind glass and handed with the utmost care. We often forget the wondrous culture that is centuries old and happened in the rich forests that were cleared to build the residential neighborhoods we currently inhabit.

In these ancient "fables" we find the memories, stories, and legends which persist. The tales that not only point out our similarities, but may also direct us to a large and more fascinating existence.

FIVE MYTHS PEOPLE TEND TO BELIEVE ABOUT PARANORMAL RESEARCH...
BECAUSE OF TELEVISION AND MOVIES

5. Demons are everywhere.

Over the past 10 years, demons must have been working overtime. It seems like everyone everywhere is either being attacked by a demonic force or is possessed by one. Talking to researchers, priests and historians, it seems that cases of what many people believe to be "demonic" energies or beings is actually very uncommon. Although the Vatican itself will not acknowledge an actual number of cases that they become involved with, by researching where and when they will confirm priests to perform exorcisms we find that perhaps the number might be somewhere between 10 and 20 cases a year world-wide. Now, remember the Vatican has unlimited funds and time to investigate cases and yet they find throughout the world only 10 to 20 cases a year that need intervention. So why does every ghost hunting team find a demon?

Why are exorcisms and deliverances being performed almost nightly on paranormal reality television shows? Mostly because people don't truly understand what is actually involved during an alleged demonic possession or when a supposedly demonic force is manifesting itself. As a side note, most people who call themselves "demonologists" don't even understand what that word traditionally means (see earlier chapter) Sorry, but it's true.

4. EVP is a relatively new process.

Experimenting with Direct Voice, Electronic Voice Phenomena and other forms of I.T.C. has been around for as long as the technology to perform it has been around. Pioneers, like Jungerson, started honing their skills and research methodologies close to 70 years ago. Even equipment like the "ghost box" has its origins with inventors like Thomas Edison. It's not a new process and unfortunately many researchers are unaware of the decades worth of documentation, data and evidence on how and why the process is supposed to work. Here's a tip: Long ago, EVP researchers determined that if you can only hear an understandable voice because of manipulation to the recording, then the evidence is no good, so try again.

3. Screaming at a ghost is a great way to get a response.
In an earlier chapter, "Come at me ghost," I looked at ways that "provoking" probably isn't a wonderful form of investigating. Put as plainly as possible, when someone I know, who is alive, starts yelling at me I'm pretty likely to not respond or to respond badly.

2. Psychics/Mediums are needed to investigate.
Throughout the past 20 years I have utilized persons who regard themselves as "psychic" or "mediumistic" to act as additional tools during research. Unfortunately, psychic power is part of the paranormal phenomena which we as researchers are supposed to be investigating.

Using paranormal phenomena to explain paranormal phenomena is like getting lost in the forest and then asking yourself for directions out of the forest. Again, I have no problem asking someone if they can confirm or deny information, but then I will have to confirm or deny what they are telling me. Then I will have to study the psychic to figure out how they have received that information. Psychics/Mediums, in my opinion, should be treated as a piece of equipment to further your research, but only after all accepted/traditional forms of research and investigation are exhausted.

1. Investigation happens at night.
Ghosts probably don't wear watches. It's more than likely that if

there is a spirit realm, time does not exist in a way that we, the living, understand. Television producers know that humans have an inherent fear of the dark, so most of the time research and investigation is shown taking place only or mostly at night. In all honesty most of the "research" that should be taking place can only happen during the day because places like libraries and court houses are only open during the day.

Also, interviewing people usually has to take place during daylight hours, since most people are usually asleep at night. On-site investigations should take place during all times of the day to allow the researcher to see when the activity in a location is most energetic... plus during the day you don't have to stumble around a dark unfamiliar house... and bang your shins, because that really hurts.

HAUNTED HOOEY

Part One: Shifty Seances

Throughout the course of my life I have on many occasions been invited to, and indeed have partaken in, séances, psychic readings, table turnings/liftings, and all other manner of so called spiritualistic or psychical events. In all of those instances I attended not only to hopefully witness some miracle of unexplainable origin but also satiate my curiosity as to how the phenomena would be made manifest. During the early years of my delving into the world of anomalistic phenomena I realized that I needed to know how I could be tricked.

The mind is a complicated but easily fooled machine and with this realization I made the decision to join as many guilds of magic as I could. I threw myself into the study and practice of illusions, mentalism, stage hypnosis and all other manner of trickery which could fool the senses and even more importantly might alter my ideas about actual supernatural phenomena.

Now, I'm sure that many of my former breather in the world of magic will be somewhat dismay at this article and details which it will reveal but it is more important, to me, to expose some of the ways which people have fooled so many for so long. I am in no way saying that all psychical experiences are some manner of trickery but I simply want to show how it was done so that those who might one day be introduced into "strange" situations may be able to truly discern if something is blatant hoaxing.

THE ORIGINAL SÉANCES:
Beginning the late 1800's séances and mediumistic parlor sittings were

becoming a common experience in Europe and America. Traditionally these séances were held in rooms which, at some point of the séance, could be made totally dark. The stage magician F. Shields wrote:

"A dark room is necessary, and I do mean dark, dim or dusky will not do. If the séance is to succeed you must not be able to see the hand in front of the face."

When it comes time for the "spirit" to make itself known it will be an absolute necessity to have a free hand. But how is this to be accomplished when hands are all on the table? Mentalist William Larson explains how to free your hand.

"Have each guest place his hands on the table in front of him. The fingers should be outstretched. The thumbs should be about three inches apart. The fourth, little finger of each hand should touch the fourth finger of the person next to them".

By doing so a "psychic -circle" will be formed. Larson continues:

"If anyone of us tries to move a hand or hands, those next to him will know. When you are ready to "black out" the room you should request the guest at your right to do so. Have only one light in the room and make sure it is slightly behind you and to your right. The light is placed so that naturally when you make the request of your guest he will use his left hand. Now, however, instead of placing your right fourth finger on his left fourth finger, you span your left hand so that the left thumb is touching the left fourth finger of the guest at your right."

Now, obviously all manner of trickery can happen in the dark since you have a free hand.

As early as 1900 "Tapping" had become all the rage at séances and it was commonly known throughout circles of practicing magicians that, as magician Stephen Trulow said, "five to six small beans placed in the mouth and blown one at a time to act as a response to a questioner can provide a variety of "taps" unequaled by spirits."

Another "strange happening would be the appearance of small luminescent lights while the room was dark. The mentalist Dunninger talked about creating these spirit lights in his "Mystic Series" pamphlets.

"A piece of piece of black cardboard with a good daubing of luminous paint is placed under the medium's shoe along the instep. Naturally this is kept towards the floor until the lights are turned off. The leg is then lifted and swung to and fro. The glowing object appears and responds to the mediums desires. The foot is of course returned to the floor when the lights are snapped back on."

Now these are simply a few of the tricks that magicians, and some mediums, used in the deception of others. There are literally thousands more with many being very elaborate. The goal in revealing these "tricks" is so that a casual observer or even a well-versed researcher of the supernatural understands that in many instances deception is more easily created than you may think it is.

Part Two: Cold Readings

Over the last 100 years there have been numerous and various attempts to gather and collect data which would prove that some, or all, people do indeed possess some sort of psychic ability. The results are as controversial as the findings and belief systems of the persons involved in administering and taking the tests. One thing we do know for sure is that there are ways to conduct what look like actual psychic readings without having any psychic ability at all, the most commonly known is the process of "Cold Reading."

Now, the ways in which cold reading can be done are extensive and well beyond the scope of what I am attempting to cover in the first part of this brief article but I will hopefully try and touch upon some of the more interesting and deceitful ways in which anyone can create the illusion of psychic powers.

Acting like you know:

A very subtle way of starting to influence how a person thinks about you and your "psychic" powers is to phrase very simple actions which the person is already naturally doing. If you ask someone to, "think of a name" or "think about someone" give them a moment and then say something to the effect of, "Now, as you finish thinking." The language is key in cold reading. You would never say, "Tell me when you're finished" because this would reveal that you don't know when they are done. But, since you've given them a command, "Think about someone who is near to you." and since you've waited a moment you can assume they have done the action and are nearing completion of the task. So, when you say, "Now, as you finish." There is a subtle sense that you knew they were finishing the task. Using proper indirect comments like this allows the person to start believing that you know what is going on in their mind at every moment.

Demographics:

The basic standard of all cold readings is realizing that humans, for as much as we like to believe, are not very different. When speaking in generalities we are often times relating to others on a much deeper level because they have experienced similar experiences. There are six key demographics that a cold reader must deal with these are young men, young women, mature men, mature women, senior men and senior women. These six types of individuals are "tendency oriented" which is very much like stereotyping. Again, we are not so different and it is this commonality that can be best exploited. Let's look at some examples you can use on each of the types.

Young Men: There is a lot of energy and desire to accomplish goals. They are deeply skeptical. They are starting to feel commitment pressures from lovers. They are looking for a "big break" and usually are wondering why everything is taking so long to happen.

Things to say during a cold read: Don't call her…Progressing slowly… More Waiting… Big Opportunity.

Young Women: They are usually feeling undervalued at their job because of this there is a tendency to feel that they are smarter and harder working then the others at their job. There is a heavy focus on professional development. They are striving to stay independent and concerned with not making the mistakes of their Mothers. Social pressures are at their highest at this point for younger women.

Things to say during a cold read: That guy… Love won't hurt… it takes sacrifices… They will see… More attractive… Last Chance.

Mature Men: They are mostly reaching material stability. There is an increase in wondering about investments of time and money. There is a decrease in self-esteem and health is becoming an issue.

Things to say during a cold read: Thinking of an adventure… It's not too late…Call a doctor… Too risky?…Need more energy.

Typically the hardest to read are mature women. This is due to the changing nature and aspects of society. There are two general categories of mature women

1. Conventional

2. Modern.

There is some overlap and so it is up to the cold reader to make the leap using body posturing, and manner of speech/ dress to determine the best fit.

Mature Women:

Conventional: There is a tendency to be slightly more judgmental about younger women but celebratory about younger women's courage. Thinking about traditional motherhood roles increases and there are concerns about health issues.

Modern: There is an increase in the feelings of mistreatment about their role in society. They are willing to explore new areas of thought. A growing concerned with partner fidelity and personal health issues.

Things to say during a cold reading: Right decision?…Hard Choices…Keeping it a secret…worrying too much…no one cares.

Senior Men: They are more cynical about the future. Health is vastly important. There is an increase in enjoying life without pressures of ambition. Small things are valued for their worth.

Things to say at a cold read: Too many places…They'll see…How much more time?…They think they know.

Senior Women: They are demanding of themselves, and there is an increase in self-rediscovery. They have pride with the ability to deal with difficult situations. Embracing progress becomes important.

Things to say at a cold read: Unspoken pain…I'm proud of him (her)…He (she) doesn't know how to take care of him (her)…living alone.

Although the above outlines are very brief they serve as examples of how and what people performing cold readings can say, or do, to influence how you feel about the "psychic" experience they are performing for you. The most important thing a cold reader can understand is that they already know all about you because they know people like you.

Part Three: Hoaxing Haunts

Since I have now described some tricks that people have employed during séances to create what would seem to be supernatural happenings. I'll take a moment to describe what some people have done to convince others that a location is haunted.

Dry Ice:
Believe it or not dry ice not only makes cool looking fog and smoke but it is also used to help create the illusion of spectral denizens. In part

one "Shifty Seances" I wrote about people using a mouth full of beans to spit out to create "rapping" sounds; well dry ice, which should not be put in your mouth, can create bumps and bangs in a much more sneaky manner. A person can carry around small chips of dry ice in their coat pocket and whenever they feel so inclined can throw or flick those chips around a room. Now after the "taps" have been heard the only thing they have to do is keep people away from the chip of dry ice until it evaporates. In some cases the evaporation of the dry ice chip will even catch the flash from a vigilant camera-person and create a spooky "mist" which, since coming from the same direction as the "tapping," must have been the ghost!

Another trick utilizing dry ice is performed by slightly compressing a plastic water bottle and placing a small chip inside. Tighten the cap and place the bottle somewhere; as the dry ice evaporates the bottle will start to inflate causing the plastic to snap and pop. In a dark location the sources of the sounds will almost never be found, especially since once the bottle fully expands the sounds will stop and if the bottle is discovered, well, it's just an empty water bottle.

Invisible Thread:
For those of you, who have ever seen a magician "float" a small object or dollar bill the illusion is created by the use of a mono-filament thread, usually made of nylon called "invisible thread". Even up close and in a well-lit area invisible thread is difficult to see which makes it perfect for close-up illusions. In cases of "haunted" locations the string can be pre-attached to small objects, like a ball or a sheet of paper, to make them move. Once the string is broken or dis-attached from the item it almost completely undetectable.

Although invisible thread tends to be very "breakable" if multiple threads are used they can move much larger objects, although only slightly, but sometimes slightly is enough to convince those looking to be convinced. I have also seen a person attach a long strand onto their fingers so that it will, when the arm is raised, brush against the face of someone standing near them creating the feeling of "cobwebs" touching their face.

Pre-recorded EVPS:

Believe it or not strange voices can sometimes be recorded on a digital recorder before they are recorded on a digital recorder! If that sounds confusing…it is. There have been two instances in which I found "investigators" faking EVPS, by playing EVPS.

What?

The trick goes something like this. An "investigator" records weird whispering words into their recorder before anyone arrives then after others get to the location and during the EVP sessions the hoaxer plays their recordings while pretending to make recordings along with everyone else! Of course the sounds are sometimes heard as they are being played so people will check their devices and guess what? Some people will have recorded them! Boom! EVPs! Of course EVPS don't show up on everyone's recorders, including the person who originally recorded the voices which were played to hoax the EVP in the first place.

If people spent as much time thinking about and constructing ideas about what is called paranormal phenomena as they do trying to hoax hauntings then perhaps we, together, could move our ideas and concepts into a new and more vigorous community of the weirdly-minded. Until then make sure your watching for hoaxes as much as your looking for haunts.

FIVE REASONS WHY PARANORMAL RESEARCH IS PROBABLY NOT TAKEN SERIOUSLY BY THE SCIENTIFIC COMMUNITY.

Paranormal/Psychical research has never been fully embraced by the accepted scientific community and although many of the people involved in the investigation of supernatural phenomena endlessly discuss the wanting to be taken seriously here are some reasons why I believe this field continues to be regarded by many people as a joke.

5. Merchandise.
Sometimes... after years of studying in their field of speciality a scientist will become very well recognized, Stephen Hawking, Brian Greene and Neil deGrasse Tyson, and because of their increased exposure they MIGHT have a t-shirt with their face or their slogan on it. They will probably have books they can sell and maybe... maybe, some other kind of trinket but that is about it.

For paranormal researchers one of the first things an up-and-coming team of researchers does is throw their logo on everything from t-shirts to key-chains and shot glasses. There is something fundamentally wrong when an investigator/team has more t-shirt and baseball hat designs than years of research. Merchandising of course gives people a chance to support you or your team but when the majority of your time is spent selling things to people it can generate feelings of an environment of greed.

4. Attire.
There is no reason a "professional" researcher/investigator should ever show up to a client's house looking like they just came from either a rock concert or a theme park. There is nothing wrong with dressing comfortably but, usually, when you want to present yourself as

a knowledgeable, serious professional you try and look like one. Sure, sometimes scientists "look crazy" (like Einstein and his hair), but think about it this way, because scientists so-commonly dress professionally, including Einstein, 50 years later we still have to use Einstein's hair as an example of a crazy looking scientist.

Of course society is changing and we all accept that people are different. Fashion is personal and people should where want ever they want but we should strive to make ourselves as serious as possible if we are going to present ourselves as being serious. For as much as we would like to believe that people do not judge books by their covers the reality is that initial assumptions are based upon first meetings and that first meetings include first visual contact with individuals. At least wear a clean shirt.

3. Outrageous Claims
"Best Video Evidence of a Ghost" and in reality it's crappy, grainy footage of some fog. "Proof of the afterlife caught on video" and it's some dusty orbs floating around a dusty basement. "Real Demon Attack!" and it's an 8-year-old having a temper tantrum.

All of these pieces of "data" and others like them damage the reputation of the entire field. The paranormal community at-large has forgotten that our field of research is speculative and in doing so has forgotten how to use words like "allegedly" "perhaps" "maybe" and "could". Using these words when posting a video-clip or photo may not make it as shocking, it may not get you as many viewers, but the point of our research isn't to be shocking, it's to help find answers…which leads us to #2.

2. Peer Review
Paranormal researchers so badly want to be the individual or team that "figures it all out" they tend to hoard their data. One of the most critical aspects of the scientific method, aside from being able to reproduce data, is having your data reviewed by a large body of your peers. Before any data is posted it should have passed through countless hands and

investigated by as many people as possible.

All too often groups will post enhanced photos, video and audio data but will refuse to give out the raw original material. This is key, and when the paranormal community acts like a spoiled child then the accepted scientific community will continue to treat us like spoiled children.

1. Scariness and Death

The paranormal community must, if it is willing to survive and flourish, start to re-brand paranormal phenomena in a serious manner and break away from the shock and fright mentality. Plain and simple, paranormal phenomena is not scary, at least not any scarier than working next to a particle accelerator or diving 3 miles down to the bottom of the ocean in a tin can. Paranormal phenomena is not about Death either. We don't research Death we research the persistence of life after physical Death. Most researchers already aren't scared but for some reason, usually to sell people stuff, continue to advertise itself as "scary".

The darkness in which many people choose to investigate is not a darkness that surrounds what we should be thinking about. Bloody fonts, skulls, bats and gravestones have very little, if anything, to do with the realm of supernatural phenomena. Even the blob-like ghosts featured on a countless variety of t-shirts does not conform to the alleged actual sightings of "ghosts". The experience we long for, the opportunities we seek are life-affirming and psychologically soothing.

The work we are doing is exciting, emotional and just may be the most important work anyone has done to answer some of the oldest questions known to humankind. But, as long as thousands of researchers scream and run and hide and pant in breathless panic over a "clunk" in another room how in the world do you expect anyone to take us serious? Sure people can be startled. Yes, people new to being left alone in an abandon prison might freakout. This is normal an natural but if, after numerous experiences you are still scared perhaps you should rethink what you are doing and your motivations for doing it.

ANIMAL GHOSTS

A shadow, inhuman and silent, glides through the night in search of experiences and curious knowledge. Through the dim-light of the moon, the skillful shade leaps from rooftop to tree branch, fence post to ground, pausing only briefly to sense that which is beyond the scope of human ken. Where does this creature reside when the sun raises its mighty light? Shall it return once more the next eve? What weird world does this creature inhabit, and can it understand the waking world of humans?

Our animal brethren, whether companion or wild, no matter what shape or size, exist in a world shared by all living things. How bizarre and incomprehensible must we seem to them. Our comings and goings, our spectacular flashing lights and non-stop, incessant babbling must provide endless fear and enjoyment for those whom we attempt to subdue for their own good. We cage within our homes some of these fellow beings for their safety.

How naive we are to believe that those creatures, who have existed far longer than mankind, need the protection of we who, not so long ago, could barely protect ourselves from them. The ridiculousness of our larger intelligence reveals itself in our ancestors' intent to separate themselves, elevate themselves, from nature, and yet within a few thousand years we, their lineage, now struggle to return to it. The amount we can learn from the unlearned, "less-intelligent" beings who never sought to establish dominance over the natural world is not only endless but also infinitely kind of them.

There is no judgment, save ours, in the animal kingdom. So, when we conceptualize an afterlife we sometimes find ourselves asking, "What happens when animals die?"

The question itself is amusing in the sense that we have convinced ourselves that we are not in any way related to all of the other living beings of this planet. If there is a Heaven, Hell, or any ethereal world after this one, we have no direct or discernible knowledge of it, and still we question whether other creatures will inhabit that veiled world with us!

I can only hope that, if a world exists beyond this one, the "animals" who are forced to live now with us have not to experience our arrogance and conceit for endless eons. In an afterlife filled by all creatures, I hope to overhear the conversations and excuses that humans will make to their animal family for the indecency, torture, and cruelty we visited upon them in the here and now.

An eternal heaven could not exist without skies colored by the wings of birds, the care and concern of canines, the playful curiosity of kittens, the majesty of elephants, the delicateness of the insect kingdom, and all the other inexplicable marvels of creatures other than man. If there is no afterlife, if this world is all there is, then we, as its self-proclaimed keepers, should take the time to appreciate how heavenly it has been made by those we seek to elevate ourselves over. And if there is indeed a eternal Heaven of everlasting peace it could not be so if it were not populated by those beings who are the better parts of ourselves.

IT'S FINE TO JUST LIKE WEIRD THINGS

Throughout my adult life I've watched a lot of people come into and go out of the world of researching anomalistic phenomena. Some people have an interest sparked by a movie or book and delve deeper into the high strangeness — others have a personal experience that they hope will be validated. Many come into the field with high hopes and grand expectations as to what they will discover or experience.

Over time interest fades for many or, like with any idea, excitement waxes and wanes over time and eventually the day-to-day world with its concerns overrides a once awe-filled fascination. A large number of people become dis hearted by the lack of experiences or information and become ardent cynics of that which they once believed to be real. Many find a fulfillment to their experiences and fall over the cliff into a concrete system of beliefs from which new ideas are rigorously ejected.

One of the many problems with any interest is that very few people actually realize that it's fine to just like things.

As an example I like cooking but I have no interest in becoming a chef. I like children but have little to any interest in becoming a parent. Were I to try and immerse myself into everything which I liked I would end up not being able to fully and truly like anything. How could I read, write, cook, parent, exercise, work, play all at the level which my likes demanded? There truly aren't enough hours in the day.

Wanting to more deeply explore the questions of life and death, mysterious creatures and extraterrestrials is fantastic; but you don't have to devote your life to it. You don't even have to join a group and sink thousands of dollars into any hobby. It's fine to just like things.

MODERN DAY MAGIC

It's more than common for people these days to speak of magic and want to practice magic and almost always they are convinced that they need to burn candles at midnight with crystals awash in the river water cleared by a full moon. Which is fine. ha-ha, but practical magic which is practiced everyday and in a far more subversive way, to me is much more interesting.

One of the main difficulties in discussing magic and already I have to clarify that I'm not speaking about prestidigitation, slight of hand, stage magic but the more traditional idea of magic as in spell casting is that as ideas evolve and as our understanding of human-nature, psychology and physical sciences grow magic seems to become less magically than first thought or at the least it becomes a more common knowledge and seems to be, at first glance less startling than it once was thought of.

But indeed magic, spell casting magic of what was once understood to be of the occult variety is still very much in play and practiced all over the world by individuals, corporations, governments, etcetera ad nauseam. But because of our modern day understanding of what the practice of magic has come to be recognized as we overlook the fact that magic is indeed being practiced and influencing the world everyday in a variety of ways.

One of the more curious aspects of modern magic and one that is often brushed of as some kind of irrational lunacy by larger audiences is the practice of magical systems in advertising. Now I'm sure some people have seen videos or read articles about the witchcraft or occult systems trying to slip messages into music recordings, a performers appearance at a half-time show or symbology that a director will place in a movie. Mostly these are non-purposeful aspects which by their nature have, solely by being interesting imagery or sounds, found their way into a larger piece of artistry but in many cases these images and sounds are willful manipulation and literal crafting.

To clarify and properly express what I mean by spell casting and other forms magic which people have tried to use in the alleged influencing of the outside materialistic world we have to understand what that type of magic actually is and what it involves. Modern magic is no different than what we commonly refer to as ancient or traditional magic. It is in short, the usage of words and shapes, symbols and sometimes physical actions to alter by an individual or group of individuals to exact change in someone, something or reality itself. The practicing and repeated routine is found to tie into anthropological views of Rituals which form a reverence and connection to the idealized state desired by the practitioner.

The argument can be made that Modern magic is no longer magic because it is so often practiced by people who in most cases do not know they are even performing a magical rite. But this has always been the case. Magic is a natural outgrowth of using language and imagery to affect change. Magic has always been practiced y those who are simply being human and going through the actions of living a normal human life. It is the purposeful the willful practice of Magic that the majority of people find most interesting.

Magical practice has become so common place It is literally happening so much and on such a large scale it becomes difficult to even recognize. Which is amusing because one of the most ancient occult secrets is to hide something of importance in place sight. An example of modern day magic as performed around the United States mostly by enormous groups of people happens during sporting events.

Let's take a look at any random football game.

Two small elite groups of individuals with a two different desired goals, no pun intended, are placed on a piece of ground, which in most cases have pertinent symbols or shapes placed on them. Each of these two groups have coaches, or elders who designate secret plans to disengage the secret plans of the other group and that groups elders/coaches. A time limit is set for each coordinated movement and according to the various rules/regulations the "game" begins. These games usually involve the transmission of information down a hierarchal ladder elders/ acolytes/initiates/players so that the predetermined goal can be reached.

Already we can see that not only is magic a game but conversely that games at their heart are magic. But it doesn't stop with the players of the game. Where the folkloric/ritualist magic comes into play is put into action by the fans/spectators.

The game begins, and almost immediately we begin to hear the chanting of a players name or a cities name, a "fight song" is played. The rival factions within the crowd begin to sing and chant in unison to not only show support for the team which they believe in but, in a totally unconscious way, subtly influence how the outcome of the game will be determined. Various people are wearing lucky shirts, holding lucking talisman, saying prayers; they've showed up at the event after not shaving or performing some other ritual which they hope will have an influence in benefit of the group for which they feel most attached to. These people are practicing a certain level of sympathetic magic hurling prayers and curses at other individuals in the hopes of effecting change. And indeed in some cases the "roar" of the crowd can motivate the players of the field, empowering them to a state which, alone in a field, they perhaps could not have reached.

Of course I could be just picking and choosing pertinent information to express my point but the reality is that the human brain responses to and searches for patterns. It is a pattern recognition machine and in being so loves to interact and resolve pattens which is why certain images, sounds and the way they can be manipulated can be used in the manipulation of the brain and its inner workings.

This is of course a very low-level and as stated unconscious or natural magic which occurs normally due to the human condition.

There is of course magic usage which is done purposefully and in a way which is meant to motivate or suppress ideas or actions which is far more organized and occult-like in that it involves people who are willfully trying to gain a desired out come on a larger population who do not understand they are being practiced upon.

Again, before we proceed we must understand that Magic as it was commonly and formerly known has been made to seem useless and foolish, that magic is something uneducated and simple-minded folk practiced or believed in. Yet all of the same practices and rituals are in place today but called something different and or recognized as a skill set or experience which has been un-associated to its magical parentage.

If I were to sit down with a small group of people and we discussed how best to influence 1 person or 1 million people through the use of symbols, words, tones and colors. Knowing full well we could literally make someone like something which they had previously not liked or not known about this would be akin to magic. It is now, in most cases more commonly know as advertising. Wither it be the power symbols or sigils, embedded into the collective minds of humanity like the Nike shwoosh or McDonald arches. We are in fact dealing with the same art form once understood by the so-called common-folk as magic. In the past magic/advertising/spell casting/ was understood at a deep level by the educated classes or priests, scholars or holy men. They used every word, action, inaction symbol or sound to change how or why the masses felt a certain way about a certain thing. Whether it was embedding an image or icon of suffering or hope or both, into the general populations minds was a process passed down to generations of the initiated so that control could be fixed by a few over the many.

The nature of the human animal, indeed of all animals, is reactionary. Something happens and a response occurs. Magic in the form of advertising is to ensure that the response to the action is the one which is desired by those who in most cases also have done something to create the action. Make no mistake Magic is being practiced upon all of us all of the time. For the jingles we here on the radio to the imagery during commercials. No one ever asked the general public "Please freely promote our product" and yet the majority of a person's casual wardrobe is simply a billboard for a producer or a brand.

Make no mistake the corporations of the world are spell-casting more than they ever have been. And although the genie is out of the bottle on the lower level trade-secrets of advertising, language patterns, color schemes, complimentary tones which are readily used by the general public world wide this doesn't mean that there are not, and always will be high level Magus Negotium who are influencing more than you could ever imagine.

I AM A CONSPIRACY THEORIST

The statement will not be startling to those who know me. For decades I have privately and publicly spoken to thousands of people on matters that to many seem somewhat insane. I do not believe in many of the theories that I speak about. I have been and will be fascinated by the thought process, creation of and continuation of conspiracy theories.

My goal as a theorist, archivist, researcher has been to share differing ideas on historical events so that a larger group of people may be able to lift the veil on misunderstood and controversial topics. I also hope that in the process of speaking to people, since I by no means believe that I have all the answers, together we can construct new and wonderful ways of thinking that individually we could not have developed.

When I began doing public lectures, whether they were on political assassinations or moon-landing hoaxes, I fought to create an air of normality in a community which has mostly been regarded as "kooky." I tried to explain, to those who misconstrued the concept of "conspiracy theorist" as nut-balls, that I was simply a part of a community that asked questions and demand answers. Yes, every group has "nut-balls, kooks and radicals" but most of us were intelligent, rational, creative thinkers who were trying to elevate the thinking of, not only our own community but, the whole world.
Time has passed.

I was wrong.

I have watched as conspiracy theorists have become insane. Like any money making venture those who scream the loudest, act the silliest and take arms, sometimes violently, are elevated to positions of leadership. There is no official conspiracy community, but make no mistake, people have become leaders. Their data may be flawed, but they have media access. They may not believe the beliefs they profess but they are on the radio professing them. When news channels, documentarians and television shows need a conspiracy theorist, they go to the people who have radio shows and media access. They go to the de facto-leaders of the community.

I don't want to be a leader. Some people might think I am jealous that other people have burst onto the scene and made a name for themselves, as well as a great deal of money, but be sure I don't want to be a leader. The reason I became fascinated with conspiracies in the first place was because I felt as though the events of my life were under the power of some unseen controller, it was actually my parents. I don't want to be a leader. I hated being under the thumb of cliques, school administration and employers. I wanted to be the boss of me, the only person I desired to lead was myself. But even then I knew that if I lead myself I could lead myself in the wrong direction with no hope of asking anyone else if they knew a way out.

People want to be lead.

Conspiracy theorist constantly talk about the masses of the population being "sheep" following the orders of elected officials or wealthy robber-barons. They get these ideas reinforced by the leaders of their own community. "DON'T BELIEVE THE STORY AS IT IS BEING TOLD!" shout the leaders of the conspiracy theorists, "HEAR THE REAL STORY FROM ME!" which is usually buying a DVD or a product from a sponsor of the radio show. BAHHH!

One of the reasons, when I do lectures, that people question me so heavily about my ideas is that the ideas I expound sometimes sound new, fresh and interesting. It is because they are mostly MY ideas. Formed by long nights of consideration from conversations with people of varying lifestyles and opinions. And when I end a lecture I say. "Don't believe anything I've said"

I just want people to think.

I do not want anyone hurt or to be killed. I do not wish death on my worst enemy, thankfully I don't have an enemies. I am passionate about my research and more so about the concept that we as a people can find answers. I do not agree with certain politicians but I do not want them killed. I find fault with certain religions, I do not want them abolished. I love the world I live in and I do not want it destroyed. Thinking is a beautiful part of the human condition and I wish more people would do it.

There is a difference between conspiracy theorists and conspiracy zealots. We should keep that in mind.

I digress. I, now, regard most of the people in the Conspiracy community as crazy. Not because of what they believe but because of how they act. Sheep may be easily herded into pens, following blindly in any direction... by they also bleat incredibly loud and most of the time it is because they are simply confused, scared and not intelligent enough to know what is going on. At least sheep are not cruel. Sheep cannot wish death on other sheep. They do not demand other sheep be slaughtered first or purposefully push other sheep into the killing rooms because they were born in a different country.

Unfortunately in those last two examples people are most definitely not sheep.

The squeaky wheel gets the grease, but it is also the first wheel to be replaced.

Don't believe anything I've said.

I'm sure there will be more about conspiracy theories later in this book.

DID YOU EVER SEE THAT?
TRANSIENT ENVIRONMENT PHENOMENA

How often do you drive the same route to work or home? How long have you lived in a certain location? Now, have you, after all that time, over months, years, even decades ever noticed a structure that you've never noticed before? Every year I am confronted by dozens upon dozens of individuals who swear buildings are appearing and vanishing seemingly overnight. An empty street corner sudden has become home to a fully functioning drive-thru bank or grocery store. A home, by the side of the road, that has be vacant for years suddenly isn't there. Now, it would be easy to say that the house was demolished or that the bank was built, in this day and age buildings can literally be built or crushed almost overnight. But what I am questioned, often, about seems to be something far stranger, something I've come to call Transient Environment Phenomena.

– A husband and wife who have grown up in a small community, attending its schools working in its civic area notice that where once there had been only a small, acre or smaller, patch of land is now a party story. The signs in the window are aged from years of sunlight, the parking lot riddled with potholes from years of use. When friends and family are confronted about the store everyone has seen it, people have gone there for years, there are even memories of the couple going there and getting cigarettes, but of course these "memories" are coming from the family and not the couple. Both agree they have never seen, noticed or visited the store before.

– A businesswoman who has driven the same road to work everyday for 10 years is shocked one morning to find that a centuries old abandoned farmhouse is now only a wheat field. At work she mentions the house to co-workers, no one remembers the house. "It has always been a farmer's empty field" of this everyone at her office agrees, except the woman who remembers differently.

Over the last 15 years, or longer, I have been contacted with more and more frequency about T.E.P. occurring. Buildings, houses, parks, restaurants, etc. seem to vanish or appear without warning or explanation. Usually only the person who notices the change remembers that something is different. Occasionally one or two others many have a fleeting memory of "something being different" but these cases seem to be rare.

Of course the entire phenomena could simply be a mental aberration on the part of the experiencer(s). Living in the same location or traveling the same roads for a long period of time can dull the senses to changes in the environment. The mind, as we all know, can play tricks… and perhaps that is what is going on.

Or perhaps something else is happening. Is time fluid enough to dissolve and make manifest our personal shared realities? Are certain individuals jumping into alternate universes or dimensions where the differences are only ever so slight?

So, look around, pay close attention because tomorrow is a different day and the world around you is changing all the time and perhaps it's changing more than you realize.

FROM MY BRAIN TO YOUR BRAIN,
IT'S ALL IN YOUR HEAD... GHOSTS!

Sometimes I just have to get an idea out and this is one I've talked about at lectures for years and still have never seen anyone else talk about it. When discussing "ghosts" I often hear people say, "It's all in your head" to which I respond, "Right! Everything is in my head!"

So let's get on with it shall we?

Millions of people, for thousands of years, have made the claim that they've seen what could be called a ghost. Over the years I've read and heard countless variations on the stories and each time I wonder to myself, "Where are people seeing ghosts?"

My question has little to do with the actual environmental location of the sighting; my concern is with where and how the eyes, brain and perception of the sighting is taking place. Were a ghost able to manifest a physical body then it would have to form a structure dense enough to reflect light making itself discernible to the human eye. Where would all the matter/energy come from to create this structure, and how much energy would it require to assemble that matter/energy?

Without delving deep into the mathematics behind it one could imagine that perhaps something like a Bose-Einstein condensate could be made by spirits. This condensate is made by slowing light down to a few hundred miles per-hour and in doing so creates a new form of matter. This idea was first proposed by Albert Einstein and Satyendra Nath Bose in 1924 but due to technological constraints has only recently been shown to work. Also it takes a lot of energy; enough so that we should be able to recognize and measure it as it's happening when someone "sees" a ghost. But what if most sightings are taking place not in a darkened hallway, but in the darkened recesses of our mind?

Since the process of sight occurs not outside of our body but inside of our brain isn't it at least a little possible that the sightings of ghosts and phantoms is taking place in there too?

Instead of an entity creating a "solid" body which reflects light into our eyes and therefore creating the visual image perhaps the entity is expending far less energy by circumnavigation of the eyes and firing the visual synapses directly. The entire energetic capacity of the human brain is less than the power of a low watt light-bulb, (20-40 watts) so the "sparking" of a visual/memory system is far less that trying to manifest energy in the environment around us. If ghost were "broadcasting" themselves from somewhere else it should be of interest for us to note that a UHF television station's highest radiating energetic output is approximately 10 Mega Watts, (10,000,000 Watts).

So in this thought-game it would seem to be far more likely that a ghost would want to expend a tiny amount of energy, the visual/memory systems, than to manifest matter from energy in the outside environment.

A vast number of ghostly sightings are of loved one and close friends who have shuffled off this mortal coil. Since these people were friends then there is an enormous repository of visual and sensory memory inside of our brain regarding them. Perhaps the "ghosts" are doing something far more strange, and intimate, by manipulation of our recognition systems. Imagine if you will that grandma's "ghost" looks just like she did when she was alive because she is triggering the image of herself when she was alive, the image stored in your brain. If indeed ghosts are manipulating our brains in this manner than let's look at some of questions about spectral sightings that would be cleared up.

Why do ghosts wear clothes?
Well, unless we saw them naked in life we don't have memory of them naked so we are simply seeing our own memory of them clothed.

Why do they look younger or older to different family members?
Because it's that family, experiencer, member's perspective.

But what about ghosts that aren't family members or friends, ghosts we've never seen before?

Well, this idea might also account for the wispy, blurred version of ghosts that belong to someone unknown to us. Since we do not have a recoverable memory of that entity, it chooses something in our mind which is most "like" them, but, in a sense, adds a "filter" to the recovered image it as not to confuse the experiencer; so it makes itself blurry, and somewhat unrecognizable yet still viewable.

The speculation goes on ad nauseum, ad infinitum.

I'm just putting the idea out there… in your head.

I haven't even got into the concept that there might be a genetic component which would make it easier for family members to see their own deceased relatives but I might take up that idea later on.

8 IDEAS FOR NATIONAL PARANORMAL HOLIDAYS

There are, of course, thousands of incidents I could have chosen for these holiday ideas, but I've tried to pick events which are not state specific and span across much of, if not all of, the United States. Some of these proposed holidays are serious, some are not, any of them would be great! There are many unofficial holidays but at some point I would love to see the masses of paranormal-minded people come together and create a true weird National Holiday. If Secretary's Day can be a real thing how about giving Bigfoot a nod?

8. June 24, 1947
FLYING SAUCER DAY
In celebration of Kenneth Arnold's report of seeing 9 strange flying objects, erroneously reported as "saucers" near Mount Rainer in Washington state and sparking a massive flap of UFO sightings.

7. July 8, 1947
UFO DAY
Although the Roswell incident may have occurred on June 14, 1947, on this day in July The Roswell Daily Record reported that the RAAF had captured a "Flying Saucer". Added to the sighting by Kenneth Arnold earlier in June of 1947 this has become a defining moment in UFOlore.

6. October 20, 1967
BIGFOOT DAY
It was sometime in the afternoon on this day when Roger Patterson and Robert Gimlin shot the most famous and controversial footage of a large unknown crypid. The footage to this day stirs debate about the existence of a large, as of yet, undiscovered upright-walking primate. Although reports of "Bigfoot" type creatures go back centuries this was

an earth-shaking moment in cryptozoological research.

5. March 31, 1848
SPLITFOOT DAY

Although there are many and varying accounts of what actually happened with the spirit "rappings" that took place in the home of the Fox sisters, it cannot be denied that their story influenced the wave of spiritualism which had been growing in the United States. The spirit "Mr. Splitfoot" (the Devil) was allegedly the creator of the sounds the girls heard, and although in later years the girls admitted to some hoaxing, there can be no doubt that they left a firm impression on Americans' social awareness of a psychical world.

4. October 5, 1967
CATTLE DAY

On this day the Associated Press ran a story about the cattle mutilations happening in and around Colorado. Although strange happenings have been reported for decades, this story sparked the nation's collective imagination and so began the wave of cattle/livestock mutilations that are reported to continue to this day. Everything from UFO's and secret government projects to simple animal attacks have been proposed as explanations. Many people even believe it to be one of the strangest phenomena to continually occur in the United States. Plus we should honor all those poor cows.

3. September 19–20, 1961
ABDUCTEE DAY

The reported contact and or abduction of people by so-called extraterrestrials has been reported for decades, but on the night of September 19, 1967 the experiences of Betty & Barney Hill awoke the nation's interest in the abduction phenomena. Though the events of that night remain controversial and are ascribed by many as being due to lack of sleep, stress, and false memories 'recovered' under hypnosis, the influence of the Hills on our nation's psyche remains to this day.

2. July 1856
MAD SCIENTIST MONTH

Although the world has experienced thousands of "Mad Scientists" over the centuries, none have influenced the paranormal community as much as Nikola Tesla. To this day Tesla is associated with everything from Death Rays to The 1908 Tunguska event in Russia, conspiracy theorists associate his work with the H.A.A.R.P. program as well as free energy theories, and some even believe that Mr. Tesla was not from Earth!

1. September 22, 1692
REMEMBRANCE DAY

Although the dates of those murdered during the Witch Trials are many, it was on September 22 that the so-called "8 firebrands of Hell" were hanged for allegedly practicing witchcraft. Inarguably, this is one of the most outrageous events in American history, when the lives of innocents where carelessly lost due to the ineptitude and close-mindedness of people in power. The day, like many unfortunate others, is a remembrance of what can happen when religious fervor overtakes rational thinking

GHOSTIES, SLAVES AND HISTORY

One thing that can be said about the interest of the general public in regards to paranormal phenomena is that a large percentage of people enjoy the prospects of being "freaked out" or scared. As witnessed by the ever increasing amount of horror films, supernatural television shows, and paranormal "reality" documentaries, there seems to be a fundamental desire to be witness to that which is startling or even horrific. This concept holds true mostly for nightmarish circumstances that have no provable basis in accepted scientific fact or indeed are utter fiction. When we are confronted with true horror it is not so palatable. Nonetheless, actual horror has taken place throughout America's history, and in many cases it still does occur throughout the world. One of the most horrific aspects of human history is the inhuman process of humans enslaving humans.

Slavery existed in North America long before the founding of the United States. In 1790 the number of African slaves in the states is estimated at approximately 700,000, and by 1860 that number had exploded to almost four million. The few things that the captured and kidnapped peoples brought with them to the North American continent, if they survived the abominable experience of displacement, were their stories, memories, oral histories, and belief systems.

During the 1930s, the United States government set upon the task of collecting the narratives of former slaves. Researchers were sent out with the express purpose of ensuring that the recollections of the former slaves would not be forgotten and indeed be passed down to successive generations. The slave narratives, collected by the Federal Writers' Project, contain more than 2,300 first-person accounts of slavery, which total over 9,000 typewritten pages. Federal field writers for the WPA Federal Writers' Project eventually collected stories from seventeen states with the purpose of documenting the former slaves' memories and life stories.

The writers were told what questions to ask and instructions on how to record, on paper, the dialects of the speaker. John Lomax, the National Advisor on Folklore and Folkways for the FWP, wrote to one interviewer that he recommended, "words that definitely have a notably different pronunciation from the usual should be recorded as heard." Unfortunately, since the writers collecting the stories were not professionally trained in speech transcription, Lomax's term "the usual" was, at a minimum, extremely unspecific due to the natural varying dialects and accents of the speakers. The results in many cases ended up showcasing not only the tales told by the speakers but the unintentional racial stereotypes held by the transcribers. As an example, in a majority of the accounts words used by the former slaves such as "they," "them," and "those" were recorded as "dey," "dem," and "dose."

Some of the stories and recollections told by former American slaves may sound familiar; this, I feel, is due to the common fear all humans share of the unknown. As with any collection of folktales or anecdotal stories, we find certain aspects that are repeated by various cultures across widely varying times. Through the recognition of these sometimes "silly" or "scary" stories, which are passed down from generation to generation, we may find that we are all more alike then may be suspected. Truly, we share a wonder of not only this world and this life, but any worlds or lives which may or may not lie beyond our own.

EVERYTHING THAT IS LIVING IS ALIVE

Life is a precious transient mysterious wonderful experience. Anything that is alive is living and any thing living will relatively soon die. Oddly, and so far as we currently know, the seemingly endless variety of physical forms which hold life within them are in a constant state of losing the life which inhabits them. There seems to be no way of returning life to a vessel which has lost it.

Each individual specimen of life is unique to the cosmos; once it is gone it can never be replaced. From tree to bacterium to animal to human — the uniqueness and importance of each living being is not only awe-inspiring but mourn-filled in its passing away. The importance of each living thing has been determined by those other various living things which surround it. Trees in the forest which are taller and stronger than the grass under them block the sun's rays from the forest floor inhibiting the growth of the grass. Humans which have larger brains inhibit the lives of smaller brained creatures with whom they share the world. Smaller forms of life do indeed persist even under these circumstances. Moss grows on the tree, bacterium grows within the animal body.

The almost random and self-centered dolling out of the "worth of life," determination by one living entity, that it itself is more valuable than any another, is an arrogant concept developed by those living creatures who perhaps wish to inflate themselves above others in the hopes of making their lives seem more useful and precious than any other.

It is difficult for many to recognize that a worm is as valuable as a human child or that a crab is as precious as a human parent; but the difficulty in that recognition lay within the human child's parent, not the worm and in the children of the human parent, not the crab. The life of the crab is important to the crab, the life of the worm to the worm. To say that a worm or bacterium has less value because it seems to be unaware of itself is a construct by creatures who think themselves to be self-aware and unaware that their own awareness is simply the way they are aware of their own sense of self.

To understand the chemical reactions within the biological being, is to understand the chemical reactions we are as yet unable to fully communicate and exchange or construct ideas with those life-forms which are non-human and so we apply our human ideas and concept upon them. I've even applied human concepts to worms and crabs as read above. This leads to a hierarchy of which life has more important or significant value, but again these values are determined by the determiner and not the creature which has had these values placed upon it. The Universe has had life generated within it or it has generated life. It has placed no structure of value upon any living thing. All things which are alive are living and because of this the playing field of The Universe is naturally equal for all things.

Of course the argument is made by many that since we, human animals, are of a higher intellect we should consider ourselves more necessary than those other "lesser" intelligent forms of life. A more biased opinion you would be hard-pressed to find.

As the self-proclaimed "highest intelligence" on the planet we cannot even combat the fear many humans-animals have over the outer skin-color of other human-animals. We are destructive of our environment, we war over words (itself a limiting form of idea-exchange), and we kill other living creatures to benefit ourselves without need and with a cruelty not found elsewhere in the animal kingdom. If we are truly more highly evolved than our other non-human family it seems in many cases that this evolved self-importance makes us the lesser creature in many regards.

The human animal is an animal. We are a product of this cosmos and we are no higher or lower on the spectrum of importance than any other living being. Everything that is living is alive and we should strive to understand how precious each and every living thing is to the whole of Everything.

IF ALL THERE IS IS ALL THERE IS

In so far as we can recognize, all that there is, in our reality, is all that there is. The two most vocal sides in this ever argued conversation come from the radically divergent sides of scientists and spiritualists. Each faction claiming some superior knowledge of a truth which may or may not be real, or even able to be understood.

The mechanistic, materialism of the scientific world speaks to the intellectualized part of the human animal by explaining that the seemingly shared reality we experience is, like the human itself simply a wound clock, albeit a very advanced wound clock. This machine of experiential reality has no manufacturer it is process brought about by process. The universe and all things within it are created by the fundamental laws of the universe which were created with the creation of the universe. Science reveals to us that all living things, which are alive or as recognized as such, are chemical/atomic machines; there is nothing beyond that which can be measured or tested, falsified or repeated. Life is beautiful because of its rarity, but it is ultimately meaningless as everything will eventually be destroyed when the physical universe ceases to exist.

The supernatural, spiritualism at the other end of this spectrum proclaims that physical reality is an illusion. Supernatural forces which cannot be seen, measured or studied lie at the heart of all existence. Human beings are of immeasurable importance because we are the rightful inheritors of this unseen, yet experience by many, intangible supernormal universe. Souls, spirits, heaven, God(s) are infinite and the biological human is simply a passing mirage on the way to omnipresence which underlies all of known and undiscovered reality.

In this writing I will be dealing with the first idea of a totally mechanized material reality wherein the end result is the destruction of all which has or ever will exist we will find that if indeed "all there is" is actual "all there is" we can utilize that knowledge to create brief wonderful moments in a reality which for ourselves is fleeting. Any meaning we may find in this beauty is too only a chemical reaction in our brain and therefore is without lasting value. In this type of reality all knowledge, hope, love, idea, advancement, suffering, all constructs of humanity are pointless due to their inevitable destruction at some future point in time. Scientific advancements in intelligence, medicine, life-extension, even the understanding of the fundamental nature of reality is solely for the purpose of temporally benefiting brief segments of humanity for scant seconds, in overall universal existence ,which will result eventually in nothing.

Of course it could also be argued that since time is fleeting, or seems to be, and there is no survival of anything after death we should make the most out of the small amount of time we do exist. But, this again is to benefit only the larger society which has many persons within it who could just as easily argue that since there is no point to anything at all which human beings create or do then we could indeed do anything we want. Murder, suicide, theft, bombs, destruction do whatever you want because in the end it's meaningless anyway and there is no reward or punishment nor afterlife reflection of deeds done while we have existed.

If science truly believes that "nothing is everything" and that "everything" will result in a total sum of "nothing" than they should be heralding our march into oblivion. Of course they do no such thing. They know they are only here for a short span of time and so they want the most comfortable life they can have, as indeed we all seem to want. Yet, this is pointless as well. Many people do want to kill, rape, steal, fight, destroy and if is pleasurable to them now and "now" is all they'll ever have then why should we deny others their right to live in a manner that they want? We all seem to agree that certain things are bad or evil, but again, this is in a universe which good and evil are simply ideas constructed by chemical reactions inside of brains and there is no fundamental "good' or "bad" there simply is a universe wherein "things" happened according to the fixed laws of a mechanical reality.

The philosophy, "Life is precious, enjoy it while you have it" touted by those who believe in a totally mechanized Universe operating under "fixed" laws seems veru much so to be a sham. Sure, "Enjoy life while you have it, Life is precious" but keep in mind that Life arose due to chemical and atomic combinations. The conscious understanding of what to do with your life is illusory and seems to only have meaning because the chemicals in your brain are reacting a certain way. No matter how you act or react the end result is death and the destruction of all the ideas and concepts which were resultant of the mechanized processes of your biology.

If you are a "wonderful person" eventually you will be dead and over time all parts of you will be deconstructed at an atomic level and finally completely annihilated at the end of time.

If you are a "terrible person" eventually you will be dead and over time all parts of you will be deconstructed at an atomic level and finally completely annihilated at the end of time.

When the final mathematical formula is done, when the universal equation has been completed, all of humanity, all of our accomplishments and failures will result in nothing. Total sum, zero.

At the end of the day, that is what the view of mainstream materialist modern science offers to you.

Yes, your phone will get better reception. Your life span may be increased. Your food will taste better, technology will provide, through science, a seemingly more comfortable and beautiful pointless cosmically-scaled fraction of a half-second of existence for an ultimately and inherently meaningless chemical creation which unfortunately at this moment recognizes itself as of some importance...I'm speaking of you.

This is the world though the eyes of materialism.

Do whatever you want, none of it matters.

But what if there is something more?

DO GHOSTS WEAR UNDERPANTS?

Whenever I happen to see a "ghost" photograph which is proclaimed by someone to show some ethereal being who seems to be wearing some article of clothing I almost immediately think, "Is that ghost wearing underpants?"

It may seem a strange question but at least for myself it creates a unique thought experiment. If you see a "ghost" and it is wearing a dress or a suit then the answer should of course be, "Yes, that ghost is also wearing underwear." I mean why wouldn't a ghost, who took the time to dress, also take the time to "pre-dress". Although we cannot see their socks and other undergarments we can be assured that they have gone through all necessary motions of polite dressing etiquette.

Girdles, suspenders, garters all manner of unseen wearables should be fully in place on the specter. Not only undergarments but tie-clips, earrings and other assorted materials are too most probably well in place. Sometimes "ghosts" wear military uniforms or elaborate turn-of-the-century gowns. We must also assume that all the buttons, hooks and fasteners are in place on these items.

Now, the questions becomes. Where do all these clothes exist?

If we are working on the assumption that "ghosts" manifest themselves from a sort of energy which must come from somewhere then there had to be an energetic process which allows them to create a form. This process should be measurable since it would take a large amount of energy to move a different amount of energy into a form which would be soild enough to bounch the light off the subject to be seen by our eyes.*

We as of yet have not figured out how to measure this energy transfer; but we can also assume that the amount of energy would increase with the amount of material that needed to be made manifest. So, aside from the energy it would take to simply make a human-shaped body we must also take into account the energy for the manifestation of the clothing on the body. Since it would be mostly nonsensicale for a person to be wearing pants or a dress without underwear we should assume that if the "ghost" is wearing clothes it is wearing all clothes needed to make clothes work.

So if this is the case then for whom is the ghost wearing clothes?

Obviously if we cannot see the underwear, bras, girdles,socks. etc. then why expend the energy to create them, unless they are dressing for themselves and not soely to be seen by us.

See how wonky this idea is?

Suppose a "ghost" just "poofs" into existence and they do so with clothing on. Is it the clothing they were thinking about or that you were thinking about? When I wake up in the morning I make a decision to put certain clothes on because I'm comfortable in them. I don't care what anyone else thinks about how I look. But sometimes, for mowing the lawn or some other reason, I put on clothes that aren't what I would normally wear. When this happens many times my neighbors across the street don't recognize me, friends ask me why I'm wearing what I'm wearing and sometimes don't realize it's me until I approach them. So clothes do make a difference into how we are percieved.

And what about ghosts with bulletholes or blood on them, half burned clothes, hospital gowns...if you're a "ghost" and are wearing a hospital gown because you died in it why aren't you also hooked up to the IV drip or have the sticky heart-monitor pads on your chest and arms?

Perhaps someday during one of the thousands of EVP sessions being performed around the world someone will final ask the red carpet standard, "Who are you wearing?" If a response is given, hopefully the answer will be something more exciting than "Christian Siriano" or "Gucci."

Until that time we should continue to wonder not what ghosts are wearing, but how they wear anything at all.

CONSPIRACIES
SHUT YOUR MOUTH FOR A MINUTE

Almost two decades ago I decided to take the leap into politics and run for Mayor of my hometown. I had made an earlier effort at the age of eighteen but that attempt was driven more by the energy of youth than an actual hope that I could affect change in my community. The year of my second and more serious attempt was 2000. As a person who was well-known through my community because of my lectures on paranormal/occult phenomena and conspiracy theories the campaign was sometimes a bit hyperbolic in nature. Alas, when the final votes had been counted I was not elected and I returned to my "normal" life investigating the unusual aspects of our seemingly shared reality.

Within 12 months of my mayoral campaign America changed. On September 11th 2001 the United States was witness to horror unlike anything most had ever recognized to exist. That same year in October, a month later, I was scheduled to give a conspiracy lecture in downtown Detroit.

The venue was sold out. I was scheduled to speak for one hour and when that hour had expired I spoke for another 90 minutes. Only at the end of my lecture and during a Q& A session with the crowd was the topic of September 11th mentioned. A man in the audience stood up, approached the microphone and said, "Do you think the events of September 11th are part of a conspiracy?"

I told the man that I was unwilling to discuss, at length in public, the topic of 9/11 due to the recentness of events, the fluidity of history and most importantly; I would not discuss the event while people were still mourning the losses of loved one and recuperating in hospitals. My lecture ended and I returned home as satisfied as I could have been with a lecture.

Did I want to discuss the events of September 11th during that lecture?
I did.
Did I discuss the events of September 11th during that lecture?
I did not.
There would be time to talk about it, later, with perspective and after people had at least started the, unending, process of healing.

My mentor, decades ago, instilled in me the calmness which is necessary when dealing with tragedy. When some terrible or world-shaking crisis took effect he would say, "If people are in the hospital, if someone is going to a funeral, keep your mouth shut and get busy doing the work of a historian. Collect and compile information so that an accurate, as unbiased history of events can be recorded. Speculate later, think deeply, honestly and remember that truth will be uncovered in time."

There is more important work to be done.
We need to take care of each other.

When confronted with political or societal happenings which seem to have curious, perhaps covert motives, the musings of the unseen hands of fate can wait until people are on the road toward healing. There is more important work to be done. We need to take care of each other. We need to be able to see events through eyes unclouded by the smoke of destruction.

We are obviously now living in a different time. Every person with an outrageous claim with a theory about "what really happened" about a specific event has been given voice to the entirety of the world. When there is a tragedy in this world, in this country, in your town it is only a matter of seconds before someone has uploaded a poorly constructed, error-ridden, misspelled YouTube video proclaiming their "inside insight" into the event.

In our rush to find the "real" answers we have forgotten that there are real people involved in these tragedies.

In our leap to disseminate "true" information we have leaped over true empathy for our fellow humans.

In our desire to be "first" with a theory, we've given into the desires of the worst parts of our second nature.

Demanding the truth is indeed something all human beings should do. But truth becomes more obscured when hidden beneath a garbage dump of ill-thought, immediate-response reactions.

When people are hurting, give them time to heal.
When people are mourning, give them time to cry.

Unfortunately the tragedies that happen will never go away… which means we have time to wait before we open our big mouths.

STAND UP FOR ALL WEIRDNESS
THE GHOST OF ALIEN BIGFOOTS

Back in the 1980's I would attend what were called Metaphysical Conventions. I would always get a Tarot card reading, take a photo of my aura, pick up the latest book on hauntings, watch some UFO films, and try to find a better copy of the Patterson-Gimlin film than I had found the year before. The tables were filled with psychics, UFO contactees, Sasquatch seekers, witches, channelers, crystal gazers, ghost investigators, and any other manner of person who walked on the highest, strangest string connected to reality.

After the convention many of us would find a local restaurant or coffee-shop and late into the evening we would sit and discuss the weirdness which seems to permeate our reality.

I sat at a table with John Keel who spoke of Mothman, Fr. Malachi Martin discussing exorcisms, Hans Holzer telling ghost stories, Richard Hall explaining UFO sightings, Al Berry making a case for the existence of Sasquatch and William Cooper tying it all together under the guise of government control.

These conversations would drift from the unusual to the outrageous but they were never boring. For a young man, such as myself, they lit questions like fuses. For every question or incident discussed ten more were waiting around the corner. And above all of it everyone at the table just wanted to have a deeper sense of understanding.

Where the accepted scientific community saw nothing I instead saw a multitude of possibilities and a seemingly-shared-reality spilling over with high-strangeness. As the night drew longer, UFO researchers checked the ground composition at Bigfoot sightings. Ghost investigators interviewed UFO abductees about sleep paralysis, Bigfoot researchers studied UFO landing maps. These times were a whirlwind of wonderment and a nexus of the uncanny. I would leave with a head swimming inside of a universe populated by fantastic creatures and the equally fantastic humans who speculated about solutions to these most remarkable of riddles.

There was, even then, those who chose not to cross the bridges which may connect weirdness to itself.

UFO researchers, who having a background in the hard sciences, would not discuss "giant apes". Naturalists, who while looking for "hidden hominds," would scoff at psychic phenomena. Ghost researchers who waved away flying saucers to make room for floating ghosts. They took their research seriously, but only their own research. To them everything outside of what they believed was nonsense. There was a split in the weirdness.

Over the years the communities broken further and further apart. Conventions started focusing on one aspect of the strange or another. Metaphysical conventions became Psychic Fairs, there were UFO Conventions, Bigfoot Conventions, Ghost Conferences and many times at each of these events the other events were scoffed at and disregarded.

Although there will always be some who challenge the idea that these strange events are individual in nature the predominate thought is that these strange phenomena are indeed unrelated. The beliefs are basically the same for each of the three major groups of the interested.

Bigfoot researchers are looking for an animal. It is physical and it exists. It is natural and can be caught.

Ghost researchers are looking for ghosts. They are physical, sometimes, and they exist. They are natural and can be experienced.

UFO researchers are looking for aliens. They are physical, they exist. They are natural and can be experienced and caught.

The arguments between each of the groups are also basically the same.

Ghosts and Aliens aren't real.
Aliens and Bigfoot aren't real
Bigfoot and Ghosts aren't real.

Of course the Skeptical community jumps right in and says, "None of it is real." and then they easily point to the lack of quantifiable, falsifiable, reproducible data as proof that all three groups are deluded, mistaken and full of crackpots.

The anger that some researchers, in any of the speculative fields mentioned, might feel towards Skeptics is also shared by them. Most Bigfoot researchers are skeptics of ghosts and UFOs, Most UFO researchers are skeptics of Bigfoot and ghosts. Most Ghost researchers are skeptics of Bigfoot and UFOs. And yet, all those groups constantly rant and rave against Skeptics when their particular group is attacked or threatened.

Personally, I am skeptical of all the phenomena.
I'm even skeptical of Skeptics.

What I miss are the creative open-minded, philosophical discussions of the nature of our reality and the weirdness that it seems to contain.

It's easy to say something is something as long as that something relates to the something you believe in.

This means though that a person needs to be actually open to differing ideas and what might seem to be contrarian modes of thought. What's hard to say is that you might be wrong. People want to be right, they want to know what they are talking about. They see not-knowing and being wrong as a sign of weakness.

The reality is that not-knowing leads to understanding.

Is there a Bigfoot? Are there ghosts? Do Aliens exist? Is Bigfoot an alien ghost?

I don't know.

But I will study and research every angle, I will listen to and explore every uncanny avenue with as much passion as possible... because I still want to understand.

I suggest you do the same.

What you think is weird is weirder than you think.

GOD BLESS SATAN

A few years ago I was invited to the grand opening of The Satanic Temple of Detroit. Now, I've known a lot of occultists, spellcasters and self-proclaimed "Satanists" for a long time so I wasn't shocked when the invitation arrived in my e-mail. As the date neared I saw that my weekend was open so I donned my best red and black tie and made my way to downtown Detroit for the festivities. The Satanic Temple of Detroit actually has no office or building but they do rent out buildings or use shared/donated space for events so I had no idea how large this gathering would be. When I arrived people were lined up out the door.

The first thing I thought was how much the crowd looked it seemed to be a late-1980's Goth crowd mixed, oddly, with a bus load of Jack Johnson fans. What at first seemed to be a line at the door I soon recognized as people who were either too drunk to walk up stairs to the event or people who looked like they had just been there and fallen down the stairs. I made my way inside.

Walking past people in various stages of satanic cosplay as the EDM beats got louder. I expected Bauhaus but what do I know I'm a old guy. I got myself a drink, said "hello" to some familiar faces and became quickly bored with the "70's themed porno room" and the atmosphere which in my mind was more akin to a Knights of Columbus haunted house than a grand opening of the Satanic Temple. I leaned up against a wall and lit a cigarette. I, almost immediately, felt a tapping on my shoulder. I turned to look at a heavily eye-make-upped, black robed figure whose face was fifty shades of Goth. He raised his voice above the now blaring techno music and said, "No Smoking man, you have to put it out or leave."

I stood for a second slightly bewildered.

"I can't smoke?" I said while exhaling a cloud of smoke that instantly mingled indiscernible from the bellowing fog machines surrounding me.

"No. Put it out or get out. It's against the law." He folded his arms in a display of confidence which came off more like the petulance of a child.

I looked around the room and found myself smiling at the fact that I was being kicked out of the Satanic Temple for smoking. My smile must have brought out a flash of anger in my robed disciplinarian as he now shouted at me, "You have to go!"

So I left.

When I do lectures I often stay away from the topics of religion and religious beliefs has they really have very little to do with my ideas about heterdoxical phenomena. I do have lectures which are centered around religion and philosophical concepts but these are usually performed for smaller service clubs and organizations. Make no mistake, conventions and conferences that specialize in paranormal phenomena are filled with speakers who discuss religion. Love, Light, Goddesses and Gods, are topics covered in great detail by presenters but mostly what people talk about are demons, demonic possessions, evil and the influence of The Devil. For lack of better words, Satan is sexy.

As I write this I have just returned from a convention where a speaker made multiple claims about the evil influences that permeate a building which is said to be haunted. He stated that these demonic forces are being made manifest because the property is used as a church by Satanists. Throughout this persons "lecture" I sat in the back of the audience shaking my head. The building he was talking about is fairly well-known by paranormalists and Satanists because it's also a bed and breakfast. So, with all that being said allow me to now say this about modern day "Satanists"; they don't believe in Satan.

I'm, obviously, speaking generally but, in a larger sense, a majority of today's Satanists don't believe in Satan or God or ghosts, or demons; they are Atheists. Also, most of them are lovely people.

A very large percentage of the modern Satanists I know embrace the concept of the old-world idea of "The Adversary." Satan, back in the day, was the anti-establishment candidate. Satan was a force against the progression of science in what was then a world of superstition. Today's

Satanists come from every wok of life and make up people of every race, gender and nationality. They believe in human rights, equality and rationalism. They are not supernaturalists. They do not even worship Satan.

As a point of fact, let's look at the night I was kicked out of The Satanic Temple of Detroit. Here is a group of "Satanists" doing the proper paperwork to have a large scale party and asking people, me, to leave because they, me again, are breaking the law. Those are the evil Satanists everyone is worried about? I'm more worried about people who drive 50 mph down the street in my neighborhood.

While we're here let's look at what modern Satanists say about themselves.

The Satanic Temple: "The mission of The Satanic Temple is to encourage benevolence and empathy among all people, reject tyrannical authority, advocate practical common sense and justice, and be directed by the human conscience to undertake noble pursuits guided by the individual will."

The Church of Satan: "Satanists are atheists. We see the universe as being indifferent to us...Satan to us is a symbol of pride, liberty and individualism, and it serves as an external metaphorical projection of our highest personal potential. We do not believe in Satan as a being or person."

I can understand how people who have devoted themselves to the belief in a God will find it difficult to accept that Satanists don't worship any God. The majority of this problem though is mostly to be found in the heart of the believer not the disbeliever.

More personally I have some difficulties with today's modern Satanists. I find the idea of promoting a non-religious, atheistic world view using what is most commonly understood by the world's populous as a supernatural demonic entity counterproductive but that's a larger conversation to be had at a later time while I'm sipping coffee with some Satanists.

To be as straightforward as possible, and in order to unravel a massively tangled web, there are indeed Satanists who worship Satan. There are people who believe themselves to be evil, possessed by demons and consort with creatures which they believe are denizens of Hell. This is mostly because every group has some bruised apples.

There are also a great number of these people who do not realize that they are not actually Satanists although they actually worship Satan. Worshipping Satan is problematic in many ways but one of the largest errors in the logic of worshipping Satan is that traditionally Satan is anti-love. So in worshipping Satan you are adoring him which is a form of love and therefore Satan would hate you for trying to love him. Again this is a larger and deeper conversation to be had while I'm sipping coffee with some arch-demons of the eternal hell-scape.

While I've got you here.
Let me get in a quick word on Witches.

There are a large amount of people who believe people who practice witchcraft are somehow aligned with Satan. Again, there are some people who do believe in Satan and also practice witchcraft, but throughout the decades the great majority of people I have know who consider themselves "witches" or even "wiccan" are some of the kindest, most loving, earth-nature-friendly people I have ever met. Also, almost everyone performs some version of "witchcraft" of "spellcasting". Whether it's growing out a beard so your favorite sports team wins or washing your crystal collection in rain water we all have our own little spells that we work throughout our lives, and it has nothing to do with Satan.

One time at a lecture at The Detroit Public Library a church group showed up to protest me and they carried signs that said "Stop this man's Warlockery." I found it all pretty amusing.

Lastly, if we are the good people we believe ourselves to be then we are supposed to love our enemies, so, keeping that in mind, if Satan is real... God Bless him.

DISCERNIBLE BRAINS

Brains. What big wonderfully strange lumps of goo.

Brains are, for sure, filled with things like chemicals and electric sparks but there is only consensus among those scientists who study brains that thoughts are located inside of it, and even some of those scientists disagree. I'm not here to debate whether thoughts, consciousness, etc. exist solely as chemical reactions, at least not today. I am here to examine how thoughts would interact with the world of the supernatural if those thoughts are not simply signal transduction mechanisms within that gelatinous gland in our head.

The most common form of "supernatural" communication, which is practiced cross-culturally around the world, is prayer. The concept of thinking thoughts which will bridge the gap between the physical and non-material has been performed throughout human history and in a variety of fashions. Religious individuals, many who believe "cavorting with spirits" to be "evil" perform prayer daily. If we are to conclude that an invisible supernatural realm populated by Goddesses, Gods, Angels and Demons exists and are capable of receiving our thoughts, via prayer, then it should be commonly understood that these non-corporeal denizens can indeed read our thoughts.

If we believe in the power of our thoughts and prayers, and we focus those thoughts, in order for them to be heard we are admitting that our brains and their contents can be discerned by those who are not limited by the biology in which we seem to find ourselves contained. So, if there are ethereal beings who can read our minds why do we believe that it's only a small group of beings that can do so? If an angel to one person is a guardian angel to another is a ghost to another and a spirit to another then it seems as though these non-physical beings have access to our thoughts, memories and all other unspoken ideas.

There are, of course, prayers, thoughts and chants meant to be spoken aloud. There are ancient rituals both publicly performed and sung with enthusiasm that are meant as a way of establishing communication with the unseen world. Yet it is the silent, internal thoughts that we most often find ourselves dealing with.

We have, what seems to be, an internal monologue that is almost always speaking to us. These everyday thoughts are so common and natural we often do not even realize we are using words to speak to ourselves. People sometimes forget how weird it is that we actually speak, to ourselves, inside of our own head.

There is also a non-verbal communication that happens within each of us that seems born from evolved instinct. We've learned to call that communication "intuition" or our "gut-feeling" and many times don't know what is actually triggering that form of self-communication. In any of these cases we can recognize that we communicate, internally, with ourselves more often than not.

Speaking out loud to yourself has even become the trope of someone who has "lost their mind". That phrase, so casually thrown about is interesting as well since it implies that someone speaking out loud is recognized to have lost the ability to speak internally to themselves, which, as we all are supposed to know, is where the mind resides.

Now that those comments are out, (in the aether), we are faced with the experience trying to communicate with, what people generally call, "ghosts."

When people are interested in communicating with unseen "spirits" or "ghosts" there are a wealth of ways to do so. Using recording devices, both audio and video, spirit boards, broken radios, televisions turned sideways, seances, are only a few of the ways that people try and interact with those thought to inhabit the "spirit-world." In almost all of these practices the participants, (currently in-body), speak out loud.

"Can you tell me your name?" say thousands of ghost hunters.

"How did you die?" chant a multitude of night-vision camera-carrying paranormal researchers.

Sometimes, it seems as though, an answer is received.

Sometimes there is only silence, save for the voice of the investigator asking the question.

In the majority of instances people ask their questions aloud. In speaking they create the waves necessary for sound to be received by a listener...if that listener has ears. As far as we know sound needs a receiver to be heard or recognized. In humans our ears do most of the work although our nervous system can pick up the vibrations created by the air pressure changes due to the sound waves. Yet, as far as we know "ghosts" do not have the physical requirements to hear sound.

It may seem as if I've wander far from the point and maybe I have but to me this line of thinking reveals that external sound, words shouted or whispered have very little to do with communicating with unseen non-corporeal entities. The idea, the thought, of the word or sentence seems vastly more important than the speaking of it.

I've performed hundreds of experiments wherein I have tried to communicate with an unseen entity and never once spoken aloud. I focus on my questions and internally chant them. I've gotten "responses" as often as I do when I speak aloud and sometimes the answers are more precise. Sometime I've even run a voice recorder while thinking my question, heard a response in my head, written it down on paper and then checked the recorder and got the same answer! All without speaking. It's an area of study to be investigated and you'll probably never see it on TV because it would just be people sitting around in the dark not talking.

Whether or not we speak out loud it seems very much like our heads protect our brains but not our thoughts.

*This concept harkens back to the earlier chapter in this book ,"From My Brain to Your Brain"on page 61, except in that chapter we were applying a similar idea to visualizations.

NEW OLD IDEAS FOR
PARANORMAL INVESTIGATORS

Over the years I've watched as some methods and ideas regarding the investigation of "paranormal" phenomena have risen to the top of the list while others have fallen by the wayside. A lot of the techniques employed by ghost hunters have, without a doubt, been inspired by reality television shows. There are endless experiments and methods used in chasing down ghostly phenomena some of them old and forgotten while other are being newly created. For anyone looking for a unique way of approaching investigation here is a brief list of some ideas which I have seen in use over the years but for some reason I rarely see anymore.

1. "The Circle" or "Learner Model"
Back in the early 1990's I sat in on number of experiments with what are now commonly called "EVP sessions" and they looked and felt very different than the ones I see being done today. Most commonly I came across the "Learner Model" or "Circle" session during these experiments.

How it's done
A group of people sit in a circle with a recording device placed in the center of them.

Each person in the group holds the hand of the person next to them and one person is designated as the "Start". The recorder is turned on, hands are held and the "Start" asks a question. When the "Start" is certain that enough time has gone by, after the asking of their question, they squeeze the hand of the person to their right. This person then asks the same question as the "Start." This process continues until all in the circle have asked the original question.

Once the question has circled the group the person to the right of the "Start" becomes the new "Start" and asks a new question. The process is repeated until everyone in the circle has become the "Start" and has had a chance to ask a unique question.

The general idea behind this experiment is that we do not know if there is biological factor involved in asking questions and getting responses. Every person gets a chance to ask the same question in order to see if they are helping to provoke a response from the alleged "ghosts."

2. "Flickering"

Long before the heavily debated and often argued "Flashlight" experiment where "spirits" are told to respond by turning flashlights on and off there was "Flickering." The arguments for and against using flashlights are many and will not be covered in this post but "Flickering" is different and has its own, different, debatable issues. The idea behind "Flickering" is simple and requires only two candles placed away from each other.

How it's done

The candles must be held in glass candle holders which will block direct airflow. Set the lit candles up in a darkened room and have the people in the room sit with their backs to the candles. The candles should be far enough apart so that the light from each is discernible and unique to the people in the room. Some people even use different colored glass containers for each candle. From there it's just a simple process of designating which candle will be "yes and which will be "no".

Researchers during the turn of the century used this method much in the way that people use the "Flashlight" experiment today. Watching the light from the candles flicker in response can be pretty strange and it's also relaxing which some researchers have said creates a semi-hypnagogic state which makes easier "communication" with the alleged spirits.

3. "Learned Jot Sessions" or "LJS"

Another interesting experiment for EVP sessions is performing what is called a "Learned Jot Session" Back in the mid-80's some investigators started carrying 3×5 cards and a sharpie marker when they were running around doing their day-to-day tasks. Randomly throughout the day they would pick someone and ask them to write a random question down on the 3×5 card and then without looking at it they would tuck it away. After they had about 10 questions they would put them in manila envelopes, again without looking, randomly number then from 1 to 10 and seal them up. Later during a "traditional" EVP session investigators bring out the envelopes and would ask for answers to the questions inside. Since the experimenter doesn't know the questions and no one, "alive" can read them there should be no way to get accurate responses.

It is ridiculous how many of those questions, unknown to all and never spoken aloud get answered.

4. "Proper Protocol"

Not so much an experiment as an investigation technique "The Proper Protocol" was designed by former World War 2 Veteran, Colonel Clarence Proper. During group investigations the entire team of people investigate together in total silence using only hand signals to communicate. The hand signals are derived from tactical-military hand signals. The usage of "The Proper Protocol" is a way to lessen the effect of undue influence from one investigator to another.

How it works

If three or more people are investigating a location and one person believes something to happen they snap their fingers to gain attention and then raise a hand alerting everyone to stand still, (right hand up, palm open). Then if the investigator has heard something they use their right hand to point to their right ear. If they heard a voice they point to their lips, if they heard walking they move their index and middle finger back and forth, if they saw something they point to their right eye, if they smell something they point to their nose, if they felt a physical sensation they lay their hand on the back of their neck. If someone else has a similar experience then, for instance, the two people who are experiencing something individually tell the person who isn't having an experience what they believe happened to them. Two finger snaps resumes the investigation. Since the individuals who are experiencing something tell a "third party" they have a way, through that person, of confirming if they are experiencing the same thing without accidentally influencing the other person.

<u>Most commonly used signals</u>
Finger Snap – Look at me
Right Hand, palm up and open – Stop
Point to Ear – Heard a sound
Point to Mouth – Heard a voice
Point to Eye – Saw something
Point to Nose – Smelled something
Hand on Back of Neck – Felt something
Hand up, Index and Middle Fingers moving back and forth – Footsteps
Left hand up – Cold
Left hand down – Hot
Two Finger Snaps – Resume Investigation
Try Some Old-New Ideas

These ideas have been used for decades but have mostly fallen away from usage, usually because they have never been shown on television.

All of these experiments and ideas are just meant to give options to those people who have fallen into a routine of investigative techniques. There is nothing wrong with experimenting and having fun and trying something new. All too often the complacency of doing the same thing over and over makes tedious what we at one time found exciting and engaging. So get out there and try something new...or old.

THE STATE OF THE UNUSUAL: 2018

Friends, Cryptozoologists, Ufologists, Phantologists, Ghost hunters, Aliens, Interdimensional Time Travelers, Cattle Mutilators, Illuminati Members, Taco Belluminati Members, Sea Beasts, Relic Humanoids, Relic Pizza Noids and Fellow Weirdos.

We are closing in on twenty years into this new century. Eighteen years beyond the predicted horrors of Y2K. Eight years since a dog named Scooby Doo testified, as a witness, in a French murder case. Six years have elapsed since the failed apocalypse of 2012; also let us not forget the failed apocalypses of 2013, 2014, and 2015. It has been and still is, a hard time for many. And great numbers of people still believe doomsday is just around the corner. Planet X growing ever closer.

But tonight, we turn the page. Tonight, after a breakthrough year for weirdos, our conspiracies are growing and getting crazier. Our reality TV shows are becoming more bizarre and hysterical. More of our like-minded friends are wondering if they have wasted their lives worrying about monsters… instead of embracing them. A larger number of our friends are discussing UFOs, Bigfoot, and Ghosts. And, we are weirder than we've ever been.

At this moment — with growing interest, the naming of hoaxers, bustling book sales, booming online content — we have risen from the dark corners of the imagination freer to write our own future. It's now up to us to choose who we want to be for decades to come.

The State of the Unusual has been so crowded with odd events, fascinating processes and confounding results that I cannot hope to give you an adequate picture of its transactions or of the far-reaching changes which have grown throughout our community and of the world.

You have yourselves witnessed these things, Mothmen, Dogmen, Bigfoot, UFO, Elves, Time-Travelers, and Ghosts. It is too soon to assess them, and we who stand in the midst of them and are part of them are less qualified than the people of a future generation will be to say what they mean, or even what they have been.. unless that person is a Time-Traveler. But some great outstanding facts are unmistakable and constitute, in a sense, part of the high-strangeness with which it is our duty to deal. To state them is to set the stage for action which must grow out of them and which we have yet to shape and determine.

This year has been unusual indeed. From the Midwest with its increase in alleged Mothman and Dogman sightings; to the shores of the Atlantic which has suffered so much from Reptilian Hurricane Machines, (much like Cobra Commander's Weather Dominator), the high desert with its secret UFO bases; to the West Coast overrun by wealthy Bohemian Vampires. Not even the heartland was quiet over the last year there have been so many Sasquatch reports it's surprising that anyone can even sleep with so much tree knocking going on.

A strong America depends on its Weirdos and our outlandish stories. We are indeed America's glory, and sometimes America's shame.

America is now a place where the terms "alternative truth" and "fake news" have become well recognized. Long ago our community was familiar with these ideas. Rhombus Earthers, Obama on Mars, The four day-day of the Time Cube. Although some people may say we are crazy we were the ones who, so many years ago, looked at Jonathan Reed's Alien Teleportation Bracelet and said, "ENOUGH!"

Somehow, our alternative facts and our fake news have been made to look… almost rational. When Orfeo Angelucci spent a week on Neptune his message was confusing but clear.

We must get along with each other. We are one family.

These stories, wild and bizarre, sought not to hurt but to help. In our modern era "fake news" and "alternative facts" are used to divide and harm. We, the Weirdos, who for so long were tormented for thinking differently must strive to provide for the peaceful and free exchange of ideas, without losing our grip on a precariously perched reality.

We do face two great challenges.

First, we must stop labeling our YouTube videos with the word "proof". If it was actually proof you wouldn't be uploading it as a three minute poorly edited YouTube video.

Second, and this one is the one that most people will have difficulty with. We must be willing to say, "I don't know."

If you don't know, then say you don't know.

We will grow as a community when people begin to embrace "I don't know" over making up some whatchmahooha answer that ultimately leaves no one feeling satisfied. Not knowing leads to knowing. And one of the smartest things you can say and do is to admit when you don't know.

Will we approach those of differing ideas fearful and reactive; dragged into costly snark wars that strain the patience of our twitter followers? Or will we snark wisely, using as many correctly spelled memes as in our power to defeat new pointless trolling threads and Facebook posts as a means to protect our sometimes insane rationalizations?

We will not reach that goal today, or tomorrow. We may not reach it in our own lifetime. But the quest is the greatest adventure of our century. We sometimes cry out at the burden of our obligations, the complexity of our decisions, the agony of our choices, the unintelligible responses to our EVP recordings. But there is no comfort or security for us in turning away, no solution in closed-mindedness, no relief in irresponsibility.

Weirdos of America, for all that we have endured; for all the snark and nonsense thrown upon us by social media trolls, overly self-righteous mechanized materialists and capital "S" Skeptics, the shadow of the long-held insult "Weirdo" is passing, and the State of the Unusual is strong.

My fellow Weirdos, we are a unique, loose-knit and highly dysfunctional family. But we, have made it through some hard times. Almost 20 years into this new century, we have picked ourselves up, brushed ourselves off, and begin again the work of remaking the idea of the Weirdo. We have polished the spaceships, dusted away our orbs, and a brighter future is ours to explore. Let's continue this unusual adventure together — and let's start by being the Weirdos we always knew we could be.

DESYCHRONIZED SLEEP MANIFESTATION

Put as simply as possible DSM, Desychronized Sleep Manifestation is recording audio and/or video which is experienced during dreaming. The imagery seen during the sleep state has been used throughout history as a means of discerning events of the past, present, and perhaps future. Psychology has also tried to divine if these images hold deeper and greater underpinnings to our everyday actions and reactions. To many, the dreaming process is simply a natural phenomenon brought about by the evolution of the brain. Whatever the thoughts of each individual might be we can conclude that dreams are as intangible or existent as much anything else in an impermanent universe.

It will be argued by Skeptics and disbelievers, on many levels and quite rightly, that the human brain does not emit/radiate enough of any kind of information for the process of DSM to work in any significant way. These arguments also contain chains of reasoning which discuss the sensitivity/ insensitivity of the ferromagnetic properties of the recording mediums, the super-naturalness of it, etc, etc. I remain less than startled by these arguments, as I hope you will be, about how this process cannot work… when it does, hopefully, produce the desired effects.

Whether this process works through some scientific process of which

I am unaware, or a metaphysical process or magick remains unknown to me. Since the time of my original experiments, in the late 1990s, I have refined the process with increasingly beneficial effects. From 1998 through 2003 I experimented more than 30 times and only had five positive results. From 2004 to 2009 I reworked the process and had 12 positive results, again within 30 tests. From 2010 to 2015 the number of positive results in 30 trials became 13. As of this writing, I believe, with even more refinement, I will near 50% positive results.

The only materials required for the DSM experiment are either, or both, a blank Low-Bias audio cassette tape/reel-to-reel tape and/ or a blank VHS tape, a small magnet, (something as common as a refrigerator magnet will do), in some instances a natural sleep aid, even a nice decaffeinated tea will do, but no human-made medications.
Down the Rabbit Hole

The following eight steps are the refined process which should be used by experimenters.

1. Attach the small magnet, scotch tape is fine, to the recording medium, (VHS tape, audio cassette). Secure the magnet to the outer shell in a position near the large amount of tape.

2. The recording medium should be placed underneath the pillow where the sleeper most commonly rests their head during sleep.

3. You should attempt this process no less than 10 full sleep cycles which do not require artificial alarms for waking.

4. All of the sleep cycles are to be had while alone in bed. Animals cannot be in the bed either.

5. Do not drink any liquids directly before bed. By directly I mean within 5-10 minutes of laying down to sleep.

6. No drugs or alcohol before sleep. This part of the process has become one of the most difficult to perform, for other experimenters, since so many people are on prescription medications which can affect

brain chemistry. Do not stop taking prescription medicines to try and perform this "wacky" experiment.

7. All sleep cycles should occur between 10 p.m. and 8 a.m.

8. The room in which the sleep cycles take place should be devoid of cell phones, clock radios, computers, smart TV's, wifi/Bluetooth/cellular devices of any kind, (smart watches, dongles etc.), and no ticking clocks.

DSM Results

This is a result of one of my experiments using a VHS tape. It seems to be a building. I remember the dream from which it came but have yet to figure out if it's an actual location.

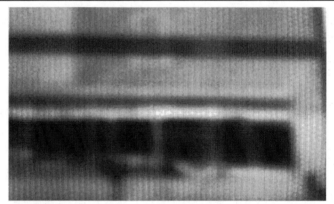

Building 4: DSM Experiment Early 2000's VHS Tape played on a late 1990's TV and VCR. Image increased in size for clarity.

After following these directions it will sometimes be found that sounds/imagery will have been recorded on the chosen medium. Since the mediums do not recognize how they are supposed to record in this event you may find that sometimes the audio will be on the VHS tape and video on the cassette tape. Recordings are usually fragmented. Sometimes recordings are backward or at odd speeds. What will be startling is that the experimenter/dreamer will be familiar with whatever is found on the recording...after all it came out of your brain.

OPEN EVERY DOOR

Not knowing when the dawn will come, I open every door.
– Emily Dickinson

One of the most wonderful things about researching, investigating and even just having a general fascination with anomalistic, paranormal, UFOlogical, cryptozoological phenomena comes from the fact no one really knows anything. Since the fields are open to speculation and imagination we have the ability, and responsibility, to look at and ponder all of the endless facets of each experience. We can use scientific methods, trace stories through folklore and mythology, experiment wildly, and debate the smallest snow laden footprint, the largest spinning light in the sky and all the raps, bumps and figures in the night.

Over the decades a large amount of "odd" phenomena has actually been explained and therefore moved from the realm of the "unknown" to a region of experience understood, now, as "known." As the illuminated bolts hurled by Zeus or Wotan became lightning there have been steps throughout history to unwind that which is not understood to that which is more easily understandable and perhaps in some instances make more sense, but the breakthroughs in science and the arts are not made in a vacuum.

For as much as we laud over those who are popularized as the ones who made a discovery we must remember that they talked to others, exchanged ideas, thought deeply and honestly about the situations in which they were mired and took those concerns to friends, family and yes even those who thought skeptically about the ideas being presented. Together is when we work best because no one really knows.

Over the last 30 years, I have ended my lectures with the phrase, "Don't believe anything I've said." I do this to challenge people not just to take the word of someone they might perceive as "learned" or "respectable" but to find the "answers" for themselves. No one can tell us our own "truth".

One of the difficulties we will encounter during our quests into the unknown are those people who "know".

Since our questions are about the unknown we often think that the answers will become known and in thinking this way we sometimes believe that someone, somewhere, already may know the answer. This fault in our logic leads down dark and obfuscating roads. When someone places themselves in the position that they "know" or that they are "in control," the "master," the "only one" who really understands they are not only setting themselves up for a terrific crash they are trying to grab as many others as they can to prevent the fall and usually end up bringing those people with them.

"I'm the only one" is a phrase bandied about by people in all aspects of our combined fields. Certain flying saucer contactees, UFO investigators, psychics, channelers, paranormal researchers, cryptozoologists, magic(k) practitioners, reiki healers, metaphysicians etc. have made the claim that they are the ones who "know," they will make the "breakthrough," they will be the one to disclose the truth to humanity. As stated earlier, the "breakthrough" does not happen in a vacuum. No one person is any more important than any other. When a person makes the transition from interested, or passionate to claiming they are the only person who knows the "truth" we should immediately take a step back and fully try to understand their motives. Fame and money are great motivators but so is obfuscation. By confusing already confounding situations a person can mire us in unending promises. We continue to stay stuck in the mud spinning our wheels becoming frustrated so that when someone comes along to "help" we readily accept it...at any cost.

When you read an article online that explains how many different "shadow people" there are remember... they don't know because no one even knows what "shadow people" are or if they even are.

When you see a television program that explains the only way to communicate with ghosts remember... no one even knows what a ghost is, or if they are, and communication is a multi-faceted experience so what do they even mean by "communication"?

When you see a tweet by someone claiming that they will be the one to lead us into a new world of "Disclosure" regarding aliens remember... Many people throughout the centuries have claimed the same thing and no one knows what aliens are, or if they are, and why does that person think they are different from all of the thousands of others making the same claim?

We must be flexible with our ideas. We must be willing to make our best guesses better. When someone tells us they "know" the "truth" we can investigate their claim but we shouldn't limit ourselves to a single person and a single option.

When it comes to thinking about strange/odd phenomena we need to have all the options on the table, and we need all the tables to be in all the rooms, and we need all the rooms to have all the doors, and we need to open all the doors.

CAN'T WE ALL JUST TAKE A RIDE?

For whatever reasons conversations of UFOs has once again reached a fevered pitch. This has happened many times over the last 70+ years but since many people alive right now aren't 70+ years old it seems that they are unaware of the cyclical nature of the phenomena.

Over the last few decades one thing that has not changed in these conversations are the arguments over who is "right" and who is "wrong" in regards to how the UFO phenomena is going to evolve.

Will aliens be revealed as true?
Does the government know about UFOs?
How long has the "truth" about UFOs been kept from the public?
How will the revelations of the "truth" behind UFOs alter and shape humanity?

The questions argued are infinite and again, not all that new. But, as per usual, sides have been taken and lines have been drawn. These divisions are also used by some as an argument for or against the phenomena.

As for myself, I remain, as always, cautiously optimist.

I'm sure that there are many people who think I hate one group or another or one idea over another but in all honesty, there is very little I hate about anything in general. I just want people to be smarter, kinder and weirder. I don't jump on bandwagons, but I don't set bandwagons on fire. I mostly just try to keep myself grounded, continue to do the work I've done for 30+ years and hope that eventually, we'll evolve enough to become better cosmic citizens whether or not there are aliens, ghosts or monsters.

Sure, I hate disinformation campaigns and not "really" knowing what is going on but I'm trying to get people to think beyond what many believe will be a giant information dump, (quickly or slowly) which will change the world.

I want people to think about what happens after that happens.

Which leads me to one of the BIG questions I have always wondered about…

If there is an advanced extraterrestrial race(s), (off-world, multidimensional, etheric, non-temporal, etc.), whatever they are and if they are here then there is probably no way we could fight them off.

They would have the technology, as Clarke hypothesized that would be "indistinguishable from magic." And so I wonder if we could not fight them, if they are not warlike, if they are trying as best they could to move us into a "higher" state of enlightenment or a more advanced state of evolution then… when, and if, we finally get to that point are we still going to stick our fingers in our ears and say "Nah nah nah nah nah nah I was right you were wrong?"

Are we still going to argue over which people were more important in leading us in the direction of a more supreme mode of existence? I really hope not. I hope part of our "advancement" will be actually getting along.

When and if we are traveling in hyperdimensional, thought-controlled ships of light is it really going to matter who was "right" and who was "wrong" when our concepts of "right" and "wrong" have become as antiquated as a biplanes?

I do not care if I am proved right.
I do not care if I am proved wrong.

I want something magical, something that makes technologically advanced aircraft as boring as, in the overall scheme of things, it actually is.

I want people to get along and to have fun doing it.

Because if we don't all get along then not all of us will be able to ride in those flying saucers and that's no fun for anyone.

THE STATE OF THE UNUSUAL 2019

Friends, Family, Ghost Hunters, Cryptozoologists, Ufologists, Phantologists, Saucerers, Transdimensional Witches, Animated Tin Cans, Robosaurians, Were-Worfs, Rosicrucians, Golden Dawn, Golden Girls, Skeptics, Believers, and Fellow Weirdos.

For those persons living in the past 2018 is approaching but for us it seems to have gone away. 2019 has arrived and it has brought along with it a surge in the sightings of UFO... television shows and new ideas about supernatural phenomena which will, once again most likely, be disregarded by popular paranormal reality shows. Twilight Zone is being rebooted, Unsolved Mysteries is being rebooted, Ghostbusters is being rebooted and the rebooted In Search Of has been booted off television. Project Blue Book is being watched by millions of people who don't really care about UFOs and it so horribly represents the actual UFO phenomena it is the perfect representation of the real Project Blue Book.

But now, we move forward. Now, we brush aside the horrible CGI UFO YouTube clips and hoaxed bigfoot reports in order to remember that more and more people are shaking of the ghostly chains of the past which kept the anomalistic fields separate for so long. UFOlogists are talking to ghost-researchers, cryptozoologists are talking to witches, and TV demons are being replaced by conversations about the nature of good and evil. People are asking deeper and more insightful questions and not expecting to find an answer but instead are looking to exchange their weird ideas with others who think as weirdly as they do – and I am proud to announce that we are weirder than we've ever been.

To those people new to the fields of anomalistic research who may have some doubts about the possibilities for advancement in the years ahead, I have doubts too but I would remind you that just 20 years ago people were stockpiling water, food, and gold for the great crash of Y2K and those fears were unfounded. 7 years ago fears overwhelmed many as we expected the apocalypse of 2012 only to be served the actual disaster of the John Cusack movie of the same name. Sometimes things get better.

In these troubled years just passed, Weirdos like us have been going through a long nightmare of TV shows about demons, movies about demons, of terrible recreations of hauntings, and people whose only goal is fame, interrupting and obfuscating the true and important work which many of us struggle to bring into the light. Even more deeply, we have gone through a long, dark night of the soul of the Weirdo. But now that night is ending. Now we must let our weirdness take flight, stand proud and tall, even if most of us are introverts and dislike dealing with other people. If ever before, now is the time for weirdos to unite.

Four the Future

Today I shall present, to our very odd community, four fairly decent goals for each of us to try and achieve.

1. Diversify your weirdness.

If you research ghosts why not also read a few books on the UFO phenomena and cryptozoology? If you wander fields looking for Bigfoot why not also wander through some allegedly haunted locations in search of ghosts? If you continually scan the skies for flying saucers why not also keep an eye out for thunderbirds? Try some witchcraft, look for gnomes, get out there and be as weird as you claim to be and be weird in as many ways as you possibly can…then get weirder.

2. Continue to not know.

Search, read, ask, discuss, challenge your ideas and after all is said and done continue to be confounded. Believing you've discovered THE answer to any "paranormal" phenomena is the surest way to lock all of the mental doors you'll need to be open to continue on your quest for knowledge. Let your "best guesses" get better and allow your ideas to evolve as new and strange information is collected and if necessary, as it should be if you are being honest with yourself, admit when you don't know what the hell is going on.

3. Remember, you got weirder... other people can too.

We all pretty much started off weird. We didn't know how to talk and we were just little crazy weirdos running around pooping and peeing our pants. Some people grew up and into their weirdness, while others grew away from it. Everyone is at a different stage in accepting their weirdness and everyone can get weirder than they currently are. Remember that we are here in this world together to help each other realize the incredibly beautiful strangeness that surrounds us in all of the forms it takes. There are some people you can easily discuss odd phenomena with, but there are others just starting their journey and they need to be eased into the odd lest they get too weirded out too fast and shrink from the ideas being presented. Gauge the situation, know your surroundings and proceed on the path to higher strangeness you'll meet all kinds of wonderful people at different junctions on that road and they all have a contribution to make.

4. Your weird story is enough.

The world of weird, odd, "paranormal" phenomena is not a contest. If you've seen one ghost and someone else has seen thirty ghosts that person isn't any better or worse than you. If you've seen strange lights in the sky and someone else has been abducted by aliens this doesn't mean the "abducted" person is any more informed than you might be. Different people have different experiences. You don't need to have continual weird experiences in order to be utterly fascinated and informed on the supernatural. We are individuals and experiences are individualized. Your story whether vast and complicated or just slightly simple and strange is important and as important as anyone else's story. Too many people, for whatever reason, start to feel that they should have more paranormal/supernatural/anomalistic experiences in order to make themselves more "interesting" so they will begin to "alter" their experiences. There is no need to make a strange experience stranger or to turn 3 experiences into 30...one is enough. Many of the deepest-thinking, most incredible researchers to the fields of research, in which we are interested, never had a single "paranormal" experience and yet they made some of the most valuable contributions simply by "thinking" about what seemed to be happening to others. Your weird experience, no matter what it is or isn't is enough. Your story is important and it should be shared without any fear or trepidation that it is somehow lesser than any other.

And I want to add, as we make these changes, we work together to improve these ideas, that our intention is not scapegoating or finger pointing. If you read the papers or watch TV you know there's been a rise these days in a certain kind of ugliness: uninformed comments, trolling, an increased sense of division.

Really, this is not us. This is not who we are and this is not acceptable.

It's a weirdo tradition to show a certain skepticism toward anomalistic phenomena. I myself have sometimes thought I alone could make a "breakthrough."

But we should deliberate, and we should discuss, and that is how we move forward, that is how a "breakthrough" is made.

And there's a mood among us. People are frustrated. There has been talk of decline. Someone even said researchers are lazy and uninspired.

Moods come and go, but weirdness endures.

And maybe for a moment it's good to remember what, in the dailyness of our lives, we forget.

We are still a tiny speck of dust in an infinite cosmos as well as a gigantic force in the microcosm.
We still really have no idea what is going on.
We still seem to be sharing a wildly weird reality that is ever-changing and filled with the unknown waiting to be known.

And we have always risen to the occasion.

And so we move on, together, as weirdos united

WEIRDO

I don't remember the first time I was called a "Weirdo" but that's probably because I was too busy protecting my body from a flurry of flying fists.

Stick and stones may break my bones but names? …well, as a society we've actually started to realize that names can hurt you too. Yet, the name "Weirdo" didn't hurt me. I liked it.

I realized that when I was being beaten, tormented and ostracized by people who considered me a "Weirdo," in my mind it meant that they must not be "Weirdos." In that moment of realization, I understood that "Weirdos" didn't beat people up, "Weirdos" didn't torment people, "Weirdos" didn't ostracize people, it's one of the things that makes a "Weirdo" weird.

We like our stuff, we like that other people like their stuff. We think however we want to think about whatever we want to think about. We don't mind that people think differently. We like engaging people with new ideas and being engaged with others who have ideas that differ from our own. We enjoy new ideas and building larger stranger and more creative ideas with others. Being a 'Weirdo" means that we recognize the paradox which is that each person is different and in that difference we have a commonality.

Long ago I started calling myself a "Weirdo." I owned it.

People in my school would sling "Weirdo" at me from across the lunch room and I would deflect it with a smile and a response of "Indeed!"

Later, people at my jobs would whisper "Weirdo" as I walked by and I would nod my head happy with my uniqueness.

It didn't stop me from getting beat up or torment but it empowered me.

Calling all Weirdos in the early 1990's when I began giving public lectures I would make flyers that called out for "Weirdos" to attend. I greeted my audiences with a friendly "Hello Weirdos!" When I saw someone in public, who I knew was a "Weirdo," even if they didn't know they were, I approached them with a handshake, a smile, and a "Hey Weirdo."

I took on the task of re-branding the word as much as I could.
At every opportunity, I would praise "Weirdos" and all their weirdness.

Some people didn't like what I was doing. They didn't understand the compliment I was giving them.

This wasn't just a word I used while talking to people about ghosts, UFOs, Ultra-terrestrials, Time Travel or Bigfoot. This was a word I used for my friends who were musicians, painters, typographers, poets, moms, dads, weirdos glorious in all their forms.

I knew there were other weirdos out there and they were doing their best at re-branding the word too.

In the late 1990's a commercial for Apple Computers came out and although it didn't say "Weirdos" the voice in the commercial spoke to them "Here's to the crazy ones. The misfits. The rebels. The troublemakers. The round pegs in the square holes. The ones who see things differently..."

They were talking about "Weirdos."

A few years later a man named Red Wassenich said "Keep Austin Weird" He was talking about a whole city, and the city loved it. Soon, other cities joined in.

When I call people "Weirdos" I mean they're weird, but what do I really mean?

The etymology of the word "weird" comes from a word in the 1400's that word is "Wyrd."

Wyrd can be translated a few ways, it can mean "that which arrives" or "that which it does". It can also mean "to turn in its own direction" or "to determine its own fate."

The word "Wyrd" was used all those centuries ago to describe people who were unlike everyone else. People who did what they wanted to do; people who rejected the norms of the day. Then too the word was meant as an insult. It was meant to make those who rebelled against authority feel weak or those who chose their own destiny against the tides of "normalcy" to feel "unnatural."

When I call someone a "Weirdo" I'm saying I appreciate what you've done to be you.

When I call someone a "Weirdo" I'm saying I appreciate the hardships that you've encountered by being the master of your own mind.

When I call someone a "Weirdo" I'm saying I appreciate all the unique ideas, thoughts and passions that you sometimes often struggle with because, I know, it's difficult to be different.

For a long time, and for many people the word "Weirdo" was an insult, a literal fist to the stomach or a slap in the face.

Now, though it can be a hug. It can be an embrace that reaffirms, to you, in a cosmos of infinite possibilities you are beautiful and unique and so am I.

Calling someone a "Weirdo" is one of the greatest compliments I, or you, can give to someone.

Now get out there and be weird, Weirdo.

OLD LECTURE FLYERS

I've always designed the flyers for my lectures. One of the aspects of supernatural phenomena that I love is the ascetic of 1950's advertisements so many of my original designs were made to mimic the feeling of those by-gone days. These flyers span the years of 1992 through 2006.

FURTHER READING

Passport to Magonia: From Folklore to Flying Saucers
Vallée, Jacques
Henry Regnery Co. 1969

The Golden Bouge
Frazer, James George
Macmillan and Co.1890

Psychic Explorations
Mitchell, Edgar
G.P. Putnam's Sons 1974

They Knew Too Much About Flying Saucers
Barker, Grey
Saucerian Press 1956

The Encyclopedia Of Witchcraft And Demonology
Robbins, Rossell Hope
Spring Books, 1959

Earth Power
Cunningham, Scott
Llewellyn Publications, 1983

The Strange World of Ted Serios
Eisenbud, Jule
Morrow, New York 1967

SPECIAL THANKS

Nancy, John, Meri, Michael, Miles
Sterling, Charlie, Sosy
Greg Newkirk, Dana Matthews
Scott Parrish, Jessica Knapik, Laura Eckert

Extra Special Thanks

Amy Wallace, Carrie Arnold, Cathy and Molly Mahannah,
Chris Jimines, Ryan Wefelmeyer, Tasma Swanson, Marle Edwards,
Susan Buckholz, Grant Searle, Jeff Greene, Angela Wade, Tonya Childrey,
Jim Dunham, Terri Doyle, Connor Habib, Stacy Wescoe, Jennifer Kula,
Carrie Magorian, Mike Bane, Michael Edwards-Ronning, Dana Stricker,
Donna Dukeshire, Jennifer Lindsay, Patricia Hutchins, Sandra Whalen,
Corinne Labita, Chris and Wes Carpenter, Jason Calderwood, Sherry Broach,
Beau Skowron, Julie Ballard, Paige Kolakowski, Michelle St. Pierre,
Courtney Block, Matt Thomas, James Rostar, Liz Beck,
Nichole Dimond, Chelsea Duke, Kristin Diesel, Karen J. Frye, Cyndi Vojvoda,
Danny Cabe, Dawn Schmelzer, Jennifer Adams,
Jennifer Corteville, Jim Perry, Rebecca Graham,
Ken Bush, Lisa Bartolone, Matt Thomas, Michele Kubat, Nicole Dimond,
Sara Schick, Toni Richards, Sonia Bondarcev, Christa Watkins

Specially Dedicated to
Shirie Zulkoski

About John E.L. Tenney

John E.L. Tenney lives in a small suburb of Detroit, Michigan.
He has been actively involved in the research and investigation
of anomalistic phenomena for most of his life on this planet. In what seems to be this
current earth-bound incarnation he considers himself to be a Monologist of Folkloric &
Occult Phenomena, part-time Humorist, Skeptical Skeptic, and Theoretical Weirdo.

For more information write to:
Weird Lectures Post Office Box 2107 Royal Oak, MI 48068
weirdlectures.com

*"It seems like what I talk about
makes people uncomfortable"*
Sumerian Proverb, 2900 BCE

*"There are children playing in the streets who could solve some of
my top problems in physics, because they have modes
of sensory perception that I lost long ago"*
J. Robert Oppenheimer

"Before I speak, I have something important to say."
Groucho Marx

*"Here is the secret wisdom.
Surprise Yourself."*
Jack Boland

Made in the USA
Coppell, TX
26 October 2020